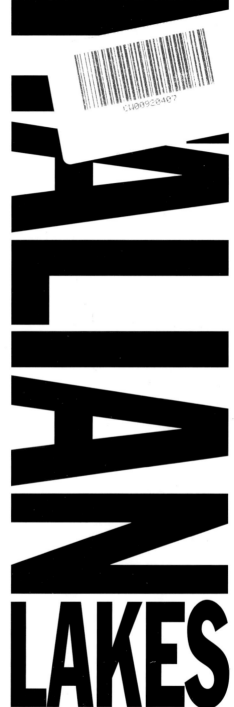

SPIRAL GUIDE

ITALIAN LAKES

AA
Publishing

Contents

Written by Richard Sale
Designed by Nucleus Design
Copy edited by Rebecca Snelling

Updated by Frances Wolverton

Published by AA Publishing, a trading name of Automobile
Association Developments Limited, whose registered office is Fanum
House, Basing View, Basingstoke, Hampshire, RG21 4EA.
Registered number 1878835.

ISBN: 978-0-7495-4738-7

A CIP catalogue record for this book is available from the
British Library.

© Automobile Association Developments Limited 2006, 2008.
Maps © Automobile Association Developments Limited 2006,
2008.
Reprinted June 2007.
Reprinted 2008. Information verified and updated.

Cover design and binding style by permission of AA Publishing

Colour separation by Keenes, Andover
Printed and bound in China by Leo Paper Products

Find out more about AA Publishing and the wide range of travel
publications and services the AA provides by visiting our website at
www.theAA.com/travel

A03439
Maps in this title produced from mapping © MAIRDUMONT /
Falk Verlag 2008
and mapping © ISTITUTO GEOGRAFICO DE AGOSTINI S.p.A.,
NOVARA 2008

In the Beginning

In northern Italy, sandwiched between the Alps to the north and the Apennines to the south, is the Lombardy Plain. This is low-lying, fertile country bisected by the River Po. The river rises beneath Monte Viso, near Italy's western border with France, in the region of Piemonte, named for its position at the 'foot of the mountains'. The river then flows east, prevented from deviating north or south by the mountain blocks, and as it does it collects the outflowing waters of the great lakes that define the geography of northern Italy.

Shaping the Lakes

During the Quaternary Ice Ages, a period covering about 1.5 million years, huge glaciers flowed down from the Alps, taking the line of least resistance between ridges of harder rock. As they advanced, the glaciers gouged out the valley bottoms and ground the loose rock to a paste, which was deposited as moraine at the sides and tips of the glacier. When the ice finally retreated, freshwater lakes, dammed by the moraine, formed in the over-deepened valleys.

Whereas the other lakes in northern Italy are long, thin and confined to their valleys, Lake Garda owes its axe shape to the piedmont glacier that formed it, so-called because once it exited from the foot of the mountains the ice spread out sideways as well as flowing forwards, forming a wide 'foot'.

Fertile Shores

Lake Garda's fertile shores and abundance of freshwater

fish attracted man from earliest times. The wide band of rich soil around the lake edge was formed from the magnesium-rich limestone brought down as glacial moraine from the Brenta Dolomites to the north. On the northern shores the strip of fertile moraine is much narrower. Indeed, in places on the western shore the high ridge descends directly into the lake. On these shores agriculture was more difficult, although more concentrated crops – olives and vines on the eastern side, lemons on the west – flourished. Today the vines are still there, growing the grapes for Bardolino. The olives are still there too, giving the eastern shore its name – the Riviera of Olives – though cultivation is now less than it was, but the lemons are now mainly a memory.

The 11th-century church at Ossuccio, on Lake Como

Lake Garda's Statistics

- Garda covers an area of 370sq km (143sq miles) and is the largest of the Italian lakes (despite Lake Maggiore's name, which means 'biggest lake').
- From top to toe Lake Garda measures 50km (30 miles) – about 10km (6 miles) shorter than Lake Maggiore.
- Garda's shoreline is 125km (77 miles), about 45km (28 miles) less than those of Lake Como and Lake Maggiore.
- The lake has a maximum depth of 346m (1,131ft). At its deepest point the bed is 281m (919ft) below sea level.
- Of Italy's great lakes, only Garda and Lugano do not have significant islands. Lake Garda has a collection of islets.
- The River Sarco feeds Lake Garda from the north, while the River Mincio flows out to the south.

Lakeside Battles

In 1842 a Turin news-paper, *Il Risorgimento* (The Awakening), was alerting Italians to the fact that their country, once the heart of the Roman Empire, was now ruled by foreign-ers. Spain controlled much of the south, Austria much of the north, while the rest of Italy was in the hands of small factional states. Spurred on by the newspaper, Italians yearned for the unifica-tion of their country but this was to take many years and cost many lives – a great number of those being lost at two major battles fought on the same day close to Lake Garda's southern shore.

A Divided Country

In 1848 Italy was divided into a number of kingdoms, few of which were controlled by Italians. In that year Vittorio Emanuele II, the king of the Piemonte-Sardinia region, attempted to unify the country. As a start, he tried to wrest control of Lombardy and Veneto from the Austrians. He failed after defeat at Novara, but in 1859 he tried again, this time enlisting the help of the French under Napoleon III. In exchange for sover-eignty of Savoy and Nice the French agreed to help push the Austrians out.

On 4 June the French defeated the Austrian army at Magenta. The Austrians retreated towards the stronghold they had created around Peschiera del Garda and on 24 June at Solferino, to the south of Sirmione, they waited. Emperor Franz Josef himself led the army: against him were the

Vittorio Emanuele II was instrumen-tal in the unification of Italy

Contemporary painting detailing the Battle of Novara

French under Napoleon III and the Piemontians under Vittorio Emanuele II – three crowned heads together on one battlefield. As dawn broke the French attacked the main Austrian force, while the Italians attacked the Austrian right-wing to the south at San Martino, a total of 270,000 men fighting.

High Cost

The tide of battle ebbed and flowed for 15 hours, the stamina of the soldiers being remarkable. But weaponry had improved since the last great land battle in Europe and the carnage was appalling. Some estimates have 40,000 men dying that day, and all agree that losses exceeded 25,000 men.

As night approached the Austrians retreated behind their defences at Peschiera, allowing the French and Italians to claim victory, though it is probable that they had actually lost more men. The suffering of the injured was terrible. In the heat of the Italian mid-summer many had lain for hours as the battle continued around them. Then a violent storm soaked those who had somehow survived. The plight of the survivors led Henri Dunant to form the Red Cross (► 22).

"The tide of battle ebbed and flowed for 15 hours . . ."

Napoleon was so appalled by the destruction that he immediately proposed a peace plan to Franz Josef, the Austrian Emperor. In a treaty signed at Villafranca, now the site of Verona's airport, he secured Lombardy for the 'new' Italy, but left the Austrians in Veneto, much to the disgust and dismay of the Piemontians. It was to be another seven years of fighting before Italy was finally united.

Wanted Territory

Though Solferino was the bloodiest battle fought near the lakes, it was not the only one. Because of its position – on the great Lombardy Plain trade route from the Adriatic (and the east) to the northern Mediterranean (and Europe) – the area had been coveted by kings and emperors since recorded history began and between

"Solferino was the bloodiest battle fought near the lake'"

1117 and 1128 Milan fought Como for control of the western plain.

Eventually Como was defeated and sacked. Power on Lake Como passed to a town called Crisopoli, the city of gold, which stood on Isola Comacina, an island near the lake's western shore. It held the lake for Milan, but Como grew again, siding with Frederick Barbarossa (Frederick the Red Beard) in his war with, and defeat of, Milan. When victory was assured, Como took its revenge on Crisopoli, invading and destroying everything – to such an extent that the town never recovered and today only ruins remain.

Venetian War Galleys on Lake Garda

In the early 15th century Milan was at war with Venice, the Milanese army marching east to besiege Bréscia, an outpost of the Serenissima. Unable to relieve the siege by land, the Venetians attempted to do so by water. A fleet of galleys, some of them war galleys, others supply ships, were dismantled at Venice, put on ox carts and towed to the River Adige. There the 26 galleys were rebuilt, launched and rowed upstream to Roverto, where they were again dismantled. From here 2,000 oxen were used to haul them to northern Lake Garda across the high San Giovanni Pass. It had taken three months to get the ships to the lake. By now things were desperate in Bréscia and the ships were hastily rebuilt. Still barely serviceable, they were launched and sailed south. At Maderno they were met by a Milanese fleet, hastily constructed there for the purpose. Despite being the superior sailors, the Venetian fleet was not really ready for battle and was defeated. Perhaps it was some consolation to the survivors of the defeat that Venice was to win the war.

The Austrian defeat at the Battle of Magenta, 4 June 1859

TIMELINE

4000BC
Early Bronze Age folk settle around Bréscia.

1000BC
The Celts and Etruscans move into the area.

300BC
The Romans defeat the Gaulish Cisalpine empire and the lakes area becomes part of the Roman Empire. The Roman remains at Sirmione, Bréscia and Desenzano are among the finest in northern Italy. Verona's amphitheatre (the Arena), dating from the 1st century, is one of the best examples outside Rome.

5th century AD
The western Roman empire falls and the Lombards settle what is now Lombard.
 Queen Theodolinda of the Lombards is converted to Christianity and makes it the 'state' religion. For her services to the faith the Pope gives Theodolinda a True Nail – one of those used in the Crucifixion. It is incorporated into the Iron Crown used at the coronation of the Italian kings and is now in Monza Cathedral.

8th century

Charlemagne defeats the Lombards and a Carolingian kingdom is established across the lakes area.

9th/10th centuries
Carolingian rule ends. The Lombards retake the area, but are replaced first by the Magyars, then by the Saxons.

12th–15th centuries

Era of the city states. The della Scala (Scaligeri) family hold Verona and Lake Garda, eventually being replaced by the Venetians. To the west the Viscontis and Sforzas of Milan take control.

16th century
The Venetians hold Lake Garda, but the land to the west is controlled by the Spanish.

18th century
The War of the Spanish Succession (1700–13) ends with Austria controlling Lake Garda and Savoy holding the western lakes.

Napoleon frees northern Italy, but Austrian rule is then reimposed.

19th century
Il Risorgimento unites all Italians in a desire for an Italian state. At a decisive battle in 1859 at Solferino the Austrians are defeated. Finally, in 1870 Italy is unified under King Vittorio Emanuele II.

20th century

The Treaty of St Germain cedes Trentino to Italy in 1919. Mussolini signs the 'Pact of Steel' with Hitler (1939), then takes Italy into a war for which she is ill prepared. In 1943 Mussolini falls from power. Hitler creates the Salò Republic for him on Lake Garda as the new Italian government declares war on Germany.
 Partisans execute Mussolini in 1945. The following year King Vittorio Emanuele III abdicates and Italy becomes a republic.
 The Treaty of Rome in 1957 creates the European Common Market, which later evolves into the European Union.

21st century
At the April 2006 election Romano Prodi's L'Ulivo party defeats Berlusconi's Forza Italia government and forms a leftwing coalition with support from the Communist party. In early 2008 Prodi's government falls and a General Election is called for April 2008.

A Sporting Paradise

Watersports

On Lake Garda, starting before dawn, the *pelèr* (or *suer*) blows from the north. This lasts until around lunchtime, when there is a period of relative calm before the *ora* begins to blow from the south, continuing through the afternoon and evening. Such dependable winds are a gift from the gods to anyone wishing to sail or windsurf. The winds are at their best at the northern end of the lake, where the narrow width of water and the height of the confining ridges funnel the air, making conditions even more stable.

Lake Garda is the best of the lakes if you want to wind-surf or sail

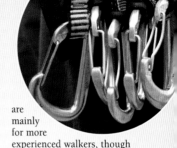

Waterskiers have more difficulty as the use of power boats is restricted, particularly near popular bathing and windsurfing areas and in the confined northern section of the lake.

Walking

The ridges flanking the lakes offer wonderful walking, though the heat

hazes of summer can limit the views. Above Lake Garda the high Monte Baldo ridge is superb walking country, but there are also well-waymarked routes on the pastoral plateaux of Tremósine and Tignale and in the Valvestino.

At Lake Como the high peaks of the Resegone and Grigna above Lecco are excellent, with fantastic views – it is said that Florence is visible on clear days from the top of the Grigna – and there are fine walks around the Intelvi Valley on the western side of the lake.

On Lake Maggiore's western shore the Alpine foothills are mainly for more experienced walkers, though anyone can enjoy the scenery of Valle Intrasca and around Monte Mottarone, reached by cable-car from Stresa.

Rock Climbing

Rock climbers head for Arco, Nago and the cliffs of the Brenta Dolomite north of Lake Garda, but non-climbers with a head for heights can take advantage of the local *Via Ferrata* (Iron Ways). These are routes with fixed iron spikes and ladders. Specialised equipment and a great deal of care are essential. Guide books to the cliffs are available in the equipment shops in Arco, which also have the names of climbers and clubs willing to help.

Skiing

There are ski lifts on Monte Baldo and on the Piani d'Erna and Piani di Bobbio above Lecco, but to be assured of snow head for Bormio.

Other Sports

Horse-riding is very popular, particularly around Lake Garda and on the plateaux of Tremósine and Tignale, and bikes are for hire in many resorts. There are also a number of golf courses, plus local clubs and sports centres where you can enjoy archery, tennis and other outdoor sports. Contact local tourist offices for details.

Taking a breather on Monte Mottarone, above Stresa, on Lake Maggiore

Top: carabiners – an essential piece of rock-climbing kit

Food and Drink

The Italian diet of pasta, an abundance of olive oil and a glass of red wine to help it down is claimed by many doctors to be one of the healthiest in Europe. The essence of the cuisine is simplicity – good-quality ingredients prepared with the minimum of fuss. Sauces and dressings are, in general, kept to a minimum, with the cooking allowing the ingredients to speak for themselves.

Pasta and Rice

The basis of many meals is, of course, pasta, but there is also a surprising amount of rice eaten as there are extensive rice fields close to Padua, south of Milan, and near Venice. Of rice dishes, the best known is *risotto alla Milanese*, a rice and saffron broth, and *risotto alla Monzese*, with minced meat and tomato added to the rice. Mantova also has a risotto speciality, a rich mix of rice, butter and onions, while a popular form in the Veneto is *risotto nero*, rice coloured (and flavoured) with the ink of cuttlefish.

Pasta comes in a bewildering number of shapes, each with its own name. Italian books specialising in pastas sometimes identify 500 or more types and usually list at least 50 as being well-known – spaghetti, vermicelli, fettuccine, macaroni, tagliatelle, fusilli, conchiglie, penne, rigatoni…To the uninitiated the array of

Pasta dishes play an important role in the Italian diet

A platter of antipasti with a mixture of vegetables, salami and seafood

shapes seems over-the-top – surely if they are all made from the same ingredients they must taste the same? In fact they do not, though the differences are subtle. The two basic forms are flour and water and egg, flour and water, but variations in the grain for the flour and the

> ## "Pasta comes in a bewildering number of shapes. . ."

ratio of surface area to volume, which varies with shape, make the difference. Whatever the pasta, there will be a sauce, the most popular being *al pomodoro*, with tomatoes, *alla carbonara*, with bacon or ham and eggs, *alle vongole*, with clams, and *alla Bolognese*, with ground meat, herbs and vegetables.

As a change from pasta and rice you could try polenta, a maize-based 'pudding' which is often served as an accompaniment to main meat dishes, as well as an antipasto. There is also gnocchi, made from chestnut flour and mashed potato, and usually including egg yolks

and pumpkin, or *pizzoccheri*, a very dark (almost black, and occasionally referred to as black pasta) pasta from the Valtellina (near Lake Como).

Pizzas

Pizzerias are found in all towns and villages. The most popular types of pizza are the simple *margharitta* and the *quattro formaggi*, which often uses local cheeses.

Starters

Local antipasti include *bresaola*, thin-sliced, air-dried, salted beef, and *missoltini*, sun-dried fish.

First Course

Primi include pasta dishes, such as ravioli – a rich ravioli of cheese and butter is a speciality of the Bergamo area – lasagne, and minestrone soup, sometimes so thick with vegetables that, with bread, it is a meal in itself.

Second Course

It is no surprise to find lake fish on most menus. There are many types, but the most popular are perch – delicious when fried lightly in olive oil and served with rice – and trout. Around Lake Garda look out for *carpione*, a lake carp which is typically fried after being marinated with herbs. Of meat dishes, *asino* is popular, particularly around Lake Orta and Mantova, though you may wish to remember before you order that donkey meat forms the basis of the various stews. *Agnello* (lamb) is also popular, and in the Ossola Valley near Lake Maggiore *viulin* (salted leg of goat stuffed with herbs and spices) is a speciality. Various forms of *vitello* (veal) will also be on offer, from lighter meals such as thin-sliced veal with wine or lemon to the richer *cotoletta alla Milanese* (➤ box).

Desserts

The Italians make the best ice-cream in the world, but if you want something more substantial there are amaretti (macaroons) and the famous Milanese dessert panettone, a buttery cake with sultanas and lemon rind.

"The Italians make the best ice-cream in the world . . ."

The name reputedly derives from the failed attempt to make bread by an apprentice chef in 19th-century Milan. When Toni's bread dough failed to rise he added butter and sweet ingredients and desperately passed it off as a dessert. It was a hit and Toni's bread – panettone – was born.

And to Drink

Italian wine is graded from DS (Denominazione Semplice), with no quality standard, through DOC (Denominazione di Origine Controllata) to DOCG (Denominazione Controllata e Garanzia), the highest standard.

The western shore of Lake Maggiore produces the famous dry, full-bodied red wines Barolo and Barbaresco, and the Franciacorte area around Lake Iseo produces good red wine and a delicious, sparkling white.

From the Valtellina, north of Lake Como, come Grumello, Inferno and Sassella, reds as rugged as the local scenery. But the most famous wines from the lakes area are those from Lake Garda's eastern shore: the light dry red Bardolino, the more full-bodied reds of the Valpolicella and the dry white Soave.

Of distilled drinks, those from Lake Como's Piona Abbey are the most famous. The monks' Gocce Imperiali

Grappa

This traditional Italian firewater is made from the pressed skins and grapes left over after winemaking. The liquid is fermented, without using sugar, then distilled into a clear, dry spirit of between 80 and 90 proof. There are dozens of different types of Grappa.

Italian or German?

One item on most menus is *cotoletta alla Milanese*, a veal cutlet fried in breadcrumbs. This is, of course, an Italian equivalent of Wienerschnitzel. The cross-over between Italian and German dishes, or, at least, the change from Italian to German names for dishes, becomes more apparent as you head north along the shores of Lake Garda. In Riva, and certainly in villages to the north, you will see Tyrolean specialities – *gertensuppe* (barley soup with speck), *gröstl* (beef and potatoes, boiled then sautéed) and various forms of *wurst* (sausage).

Lemons for sale at Sirmione, Lake Garda

(Imperial Drops) herb-based spirit is a potent brew. On Lake Garda, the Salò-distilled *acqua di cedro* is a brandy made from citrons.

After the meal, perhaps a coffee. Cappucino, locally called *cappucio*, is usually served only at breakfast. Asking for it after a meal may elicit a glance that assesses your virility. The traditional coffee is *liscio*, black and strong, and served in a very small cup. The Italians heap

in sugar. There is also *ristretto*, which is even stronger. To tone either down try *lungo*, with hot water, *macchiato,* with a little milk, or *Americano*, the familiar coffee with milk seen throughout Europe.

The alternative to coffee, particularly mid-morning, is hot chocolate. The normal form is a mix so thick that a spoon will stand up in it. If you want to actually drink it, ask for a liquid version.

From Ancient to Modern

One of the joys of a visit to the lakes area of northern Italy is the chance to observe the varied architectural styles. Though not unique in this regard, Italy is a masterclass, the competing tribes and states who came this way each contributing their own culture to create a glorious mix.

Pre-history
(4000BC–1000BC)

Early man did not have the technology to alter the landscape significantly: not until neolithic (New Stone Age) times did he leave an indelible mark.

On Isola Virginia, an island in Lake Varese (a small lake near the city of Varese, towards Lake Maggiore) there are remains from neolithic to Bronze Age times, and the Ledro lake-dwellings also date from the Bronze Age.

Roman
(753BC–5th century)

The Romans developed the 'classical' form of architecture of the Greeks, taking their style of columns and tall, open structures, but adapting them to more functional buildings. As an alternative to brick and stone they also developed concrete as a building material.

Verona's Arena is one of the finest Roman survivals in Europe. Domestic architecture can be seen in the villa at Desenzano del Garda, while the villa at Sirmione is one of the largest and most palatial ever found.

In Bréscia the remains of the temple are limited, but still a powerful reminder of Roman craftsmanship, while the excavated finds from the Bréscia site are an excellent introduction to Roman art.

Lombard
(6th–8th centuries)

Almost nothing remains from this era, but at the Church of San Severo in Lazise excavations behind the high altar have revealed an earlier Lombard church. There are also fine Lombard treasures in the museum at Bréscia.

Carolingian

The Church of San Zeno at Bardolino dates in part from the 8th century. One of the oldest churches in Italy, it is among the few survivors from the Carolingian era as later builders often tore down early churches and used the stone for their own buildings.

Romanesque
(10th–12th centuries)

The Romanesque style developed from an amalgamation of the classical with Oriental influences. In form, a Romanesque church façade has a tall central section housing the entrance, topped by a triangular section. To

Salò's Gothic Duomo, Di Santa Maria Annunziata

each side were lower, symmetrical sections with sloping roofs.

Northern Italy has many fine Romanesque buildings, but to see the truest example of the Lombard Romanesque, a much less ornamented form, but with the tall central

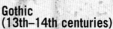

The Romanesque Basilica of San Zeno Maggiore, Verona

section pierced by a circular window, go to the Church of San Zeno Maggiore in Verona. Cremona's Duomo is another fine example. The old cathedral (the Rotonda or Duomo Vecchia) is a very fine example of early Romanesque, while Como's Broletto is the best example of secular Romanesque.

Gothic (13th–14th centuries)

The flamboyant architecture of the Gothic period was begun by Cistercian monks and rapidly taken up by other orders, and then by the builders of town churches. The greatest of the architects was Arnolfo di Cambio. Though he worked in Rome and Florence, his influence spread north and can be seen in Salò's Duomo (cathedral), which is considered by many to be the crowning glory of late-Gothic architecture.

Renaissance (15th–16th centuries)

The Renaissance (literally 'the rebirth') was a return to the symmetry and beautiful proportions of classical architecture. Palladio's Vicenza is as far as you need to travel to see the best of Renaissance architecture, but there are

other superb examples closer to the lakes – Bergamo's Piazza Vecchia and Colleoni Chapel, Verona's Piazza dei Signori, and the complex of buildings at Castiglione Olona, south of Varese.

Baroque
(17th–18th centuries)
The baroque style, with its flamboyant swirls and scrolls, was a reaction to the austerity of the Reformation. The scrolls even found their way onto Stradivarius' violins, but in architectural terms one of the finest examples has to be Isola Bella, the work of Angelo Crivelli, though the façade of Bergamo's Duomo is also a good example. This was added in 1886, way beyond the end of the true baroque era, which explains its more restrained form.

Neoclassical
(19th century)
This was another return to the classical form, but this time using modern techniques to add curves and domes. The best two examples are on Lake Como – the Tempio Voltiano in the town

of Como and the Villa Melzi d'Eryl (by Giocondo Albertolli) at Bellagio.

Art nouveau
(early 20th century)
There is no better place to look than the villas built by Giuseppe Sommaruga at Sárnico on Lake Iseo.

Later 20th century
The Casa del Fascio in Como's Piazza del Popolo is recognised as one of the best examples of 1930s (Liberty) style in Europe. Built by Giuseppe Terragni (1904–1943) in 1932, its severe lines and covered courtyard are the epitome of period style.

Isola Bella's flamboyant baroque gardens

Milan's striking 1925 football stadium, Giuseppe Meazza, home of AC Milan

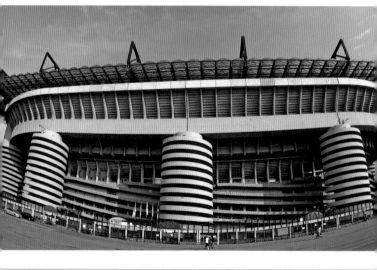

That the prediction of a nosebleed once saved the area? At Desenzano del Garda in 425 Pope Leo I met Attila the Hun, who was intent on destroying the area. The Pope told Attila that if he continued his advance on Rome he would suffer a fatal nosebleed. Attila was highly superstitious and, terrified, retreated across the Alps.

That Cornello dei Tasso, a tiny hamlet in the Val Brembana, north of Bergamo, is an important place in the history of communications? The Tassa family began a Europe-wide postal service in the late 13th century and have given their name to Tass, the Russian news agency, and to 'taxi'n from a private vehicle service they operated for 16th-century Holy Roman Emperors.

That the Cascata del Serio in the Val Seriana, to the north of Bergamo, is, at 315m (1,030ft), one of Europe's highest waterfalls – but is not usually visible? The water is normally diverted to a hydro-electric power station but on certain weekends in July and August is allowed to fall again: crowds arrive to watch the falls being switched on.

That hell has its merits? In early medieval times pirates operated on the lakes, preying on the traders who used the water to move goods north from Lombardy. Eventually, on Lake Maggiore, the Visconti of Milan were forced to act, rooting out the pirates and executing them. One pirate, captured and tried at Cerro del Lago Maggiore, was sentenced to be hanged on the beach. When asked if he had a last request the condemned man ordered a glass of wine, but there was no inn at Cerro so his request had to be denied. The pirate gave the village a look of disgust, said 'Better hell than this town of abstainers' and mounted the scaffold.

That the area has its own saint? Carlo Borromeo was born in Arona in 1538. He was a cardinal at 22, and Archbishop of Milan at 26 (though the fact that his uncle was Pope Pius IV might have helped). It was claimed that Carlo was too ugly to be anything but a saint, but he is renowned for his humanity during an outbreak of plague when at risk to his own health he helped victims. His prayers were claimed to have ended the outbreak and he was canonised in 1610. He is buried in Milan Cathedral and a gigantic statue of him stands near Arona.

That the Commedia dell'Arte began here? The improvised comedy with a cast of masked characters – Columbine, Panteloon, Pierrot, Pulcinella, Scaramouch, etc – began in Bergamo (though not all of these characters originated in Bergamo itself).

That an underwater nativity can be seen at Laveno on Lake Maggiore each year? Marble statues of Mary, Joseph, the three kings and animals are lowered into the lake. A marble statue of the Baby Jesus is added on 24 December. The ceremony, whose origins are not understood, is floodlit and attracts many visitors.

A Commedia dell'Arte character from the 16th century

Did You Know?

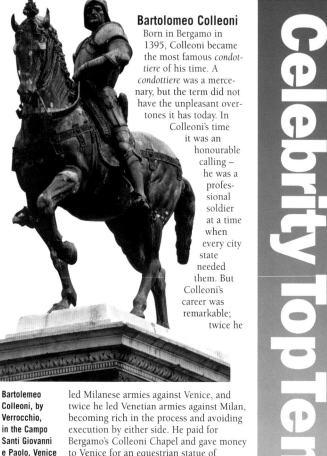

Bartolomeo Colleoni

Born in Bergamo in 1395, Colleoni became the most famous *condottiere* of his time. A *condottiere* was a mercenary, but the term did not have the unpleasant overtones it has today. In Colleoni's time it was an honourable calling – he was a professional soldier at a time when every city state needed them. But Colleoni's career was remarkable; twice he led Milanese armies against Venice, and twice he led Venetian armies against Milan, becoming rich in the process and avoiding execution by either side. He paid for Bergamo's Colleoni Chapel and gave money to Venice for an equestrian statue of himself. He specified it should be near San Marco, meaning the Basilica, but the Venetians had the last word. After Colleoni's death in 1476 they placed the statue near the School of San Marco.

Bartolemeo Colleoni, by Verrocchio, in the Campo Santi Giovanni e Paolo, Venice

A monument to the Red Cross at Solferino

Henri Dunant (1828–1910)

Dunant, a Swiss traveller, was on holiday near Lake Garda in June 1859 when the battle at Solferino took place. Dunant witnessed the suffering of the wounded and back in Switzerland wrote *Souvenir of Solferino*, an account of the aftermath, which was published in 1862. The account was instrumental in the formation of the International Red Cross

and Dunant received the first Nobel Peace Prize in 1901. A
memorial to the Red Cross, created from stone from nations
across the world, was unveiled at Solferino in 1959.

Giuseppe Garibaldi

Although not a local (he was
born in Nice), Garibaldi
(1807–1881) is famous for
his *mille*, the 1,000-strong
army with which he liberated
Sicily. Of these men, the
largest contingent came from
Bergamo, which was honoured
as the 'city of 1,000'.

Tazio Nuvolari (1892–1953)

Nuvolari was born in
Mantova and became the
greatest racing driver of the
1930s and the post-war era,
winning many Grand Prix.
He had decided to retire after
the 1948 Mille Miglia, but
couldn't finish his last race as
the brakes failed on his car.

Giuseppe
Garibaldi,
Italian soldier,
corsair and
naval captain

Andrea Palladio (1508–1580)

Architect Andrea di Pietro della Gondola was born in Padua,
but moved to Vicenza, where he worked under Trissino, who
nicknamed him Palladio after the Greek Goddess of Wisdom,
Pallas Athene. He studied the works of two architects – the
Classical Roman Vitruvius and the Italian Renaissance Leon
Battista Alberti. Palladio's masterpieces are mainly to be
seen in Vicenza (► 167–168) and Venice, and the classical
simplicity of his designs had a huge influence on architecture,
especially in Britain – hence *Palladium*.

Pope John XXIII (1881–1963)

Born Angelo Giuseppe Roncalli at the village of Sotto il
Monte, a short distance west of Bergamo, to poor parents,
Pope John XXIII was the fourth of 14 children. He became
Pope in 1958 and was renowned for his humanity and
humour. When meeting President Kennedy's wife he is said to
have worried over his choice of greeting – should it be 'Mrs
Kennedy' or 'Madame'? In the end he settled for 'Jackie'! He is
also credited with the first use of a now standard phrase –
when asked how many people worked at the Vatican he is
said to have replied 'About half of them'. Pope John became
Blessed under Pope John Paul II, a step on the road to saint-
hood. His birthplace is now a museum and a place of
pilgrimage (open Apr–Sep daily 8.30–6.30; Oct–Mar
8.30–5.30, tel: 035 791101).

Alessandro Volta (1745–1827)

Volta was born in Como and despite having no formal train-
ing in the science of physics published important papers on
electricity and magnetism before his 20th birthday. He was

made a professor at Padua University and his great contributions to the 'new' field of physics are recognised by the 'volt' having been named after him. In Como, the classical Tempio Voltiano is a museum in his honour, although much of his papers and his apparatus were destroyed in a fire in 1899.

Volta, inventor of the electric battery

The Artists

Too many famous painters and sculptors have been associated with the lakes area to do justice to them all, but special mention must be made of Andrea Mantegna (c1431–1506), who was painter to the Gonzaga court at Mantua from 1460 until his death. His superb draughtsmanship and engraving skills inspired generations of artists and some of his paintings are now considered to be among the greatest Renaissance works.

Of the present generation of artists, the Chilean-born sculptor Sergio Tapia Radic, now resident near Luino on Lake Maggiore, has attracted worldwide acclaim for his elegant works.

Mantegna's triptych altarpiece in Verona's Basilica of San Zeno Maggiore

The Romans

As well as Catullus at Sirmione, the area is famous for other important Romans. The poet Virgil was born near Mantua in about 30BC, while the writer/historians Pliny the Elder (AD23–79) and Pliny the Younger (AD62–120) were from Como. The Younger described the famous intermittent stream that flows into Lake Como near Villa Pliniana (near Torno, north of Como), and the Elder had two villas on the lake – Commedia near Lenno and Tragedia at Bellagio. In one book, Pliny the Elder claimed that the Adda River flowed through Lake Como without its waters ever mixing with lake water.

The Writers

The most famous writer from the area is Alessandro Manzoni (1785–1873), who was born close to Lake Como. Deserted by his mother at the age of seven, Manzoni began writing poetry at 16 but did not achieve fame until the publication of *I Promessi Sposi (The Betrothed)* in 1827. Sir Walter Scott claimed that it was the finest book ever written. Manzoni wrote little else of note, however, his health deteriorating and the deaths of two wives leaving him lonely and unhappy. On his death in Milan he was given a state funeral.

Of writers influenced by the lakes, particular mention must be made of Ernest Hemingway, who set part of *A Farewell to Arms* at Pallanza on Lake Maggiore, and D H Lawrence, who is said to have begun *Lady Chatterley's Lover* after a stay at Villa, near Gargnano, on Lake Garda's west shore.

A Musical Legacy

Having given the world the violin it is no surprise that the lakes area – around Lake Garda in particular – has a strong musical tradition.

The Violin

Gasparo de Salò (born at Salò on Lake Garda in 1540) and Andrea Amati of Cremona (c1520–80) each has, in his own way, a claim to the development of the modern violin. Few people, however, will disagree that Antonio Stradivarius (c1644–1737), also from Cremona, was the finest violin-maker of them all.

The secret of Stradivarius' manufacturing techniques is still debated. It is known that he searched woodland for the perfect tree – just as Michelangelo searched quarries for the perfect block of marble. Stradivarius used maple and spruce for the body of his instruments, pear and willow for the neck, but his drying techniques and the ingredients of his varnish are still unknown.

The Composers

Claudio Monteverdi (1567–1643) was born in Cremona and initially came to prominence as a composer of madrigals, his first collection being published in 1590. Together with other composers – such as Luca Morenzio, who was born near Bréscia – Monteverdi alarmed the musical establishment of the day with his use of unprepared dissonances. In

Statue of Stradivarius: regarded worldwide as the finest violin-maker

1601 he was appointed Maestro di Cappella at the Gonzaga court at Mantova and there made another imaginative leap, writing what is now recognised as the first opera, *Orfeo*, first performed in 1607. In 1632 Monteverdi became a priest, but continued to compose, producing operas in 1641 (*The Return of Ulysses to his Native Land*) and 1642 (*The Coronation of Poppea*). By then he was 75 years old.

Born into a poor family in Bergamo's Città Alta in 1797, Gaetano Donizetti was educated at a charitable school that supplied choristers to Bergamo Cathedral. When his musical talent was recognised, he was sent to study music at Bologna. His first opera was produced in Rome when he was only 25 and for the next 20 years he was the darling of the Italian theatre, writing works for opera houses all over the country to great musical acclaim. Only in 1842, when Verdi's *Nabucco* was performed, did Donizetti's pre-eminence begin to decline. But by then his health was also failing and he returned to Bergamo, where he died in 1848. There is a memorial to him in the Church of Santa Maria Maggiore.

Mention must also be made of Giuseppe Verdi (1813–1901) for although he was not born in the area he composed *La Traviata* while staying near Cadenabbia on Lake Como, and set *Rigoletto* close to Mantova. Verdi was also important during the Risorgimento, when his name was seen as a short form for 'Vittorio Emanuele, Re d'Italia' (King of Italy) and 'Viva Verdi' was written on buildings all across the lakes area.

Crowds gather for Verdi's funeral in 1901

The opera season at Verona's Arena maintains the area's prominence in classical music

Peace and Quiet

The development of the narrow flat shore line around the lakes may seem to provide limited chances for wildlife to flourish, but that is only partially true and the high ridges around the lakes are still wild, natural places.

Lakes

Above the lakeside towns and villages black kites work the updraft where lake winds meet rising grounds, their forked tails prominent.

On the lakes themselves birdlife is mainly confined to black-headed gulls and mallards. Indeed, so numerous have mallards become that you are encouraged not to feed them.

Inflowing streams to the lakes are often the haunt of kingfishers, but the real prize for the bird-lover will be the wallcreeper, with its grey body and pink wings, which can be found on lakeside rocks and also on higher ground.

At the lake edge look out for butterflies attracted by the sun and the prolific flowers. The magnificent swallowtail is one distinctive species that might be seen.

Lake Marshes

Areas of marshland near the outflowing rivers are the haunt of waterfowl and waders. These regions include the Brabbia Marsh near Lake Varese, where great reed warblers and marsh warblers breed and little crake and the water rail live. Brabbia also has its own heronry, with more than 100 breeding pairs of purple herons, grey herons and night herons.

Other areas good for birdlife are the marshlands beside the Ticino River as it leaves Lake Maggiore; and the Sebino/Torbiere bog at Lake Iseo's southern edge.

At the northern end of Lake Como the Piano de Spagna sits adjacent to the

Tengmalm's owl and swallowtail butterfly

A purple heron calling in June

inflowing Mera and Adda rivers. This area is especially important as it is not only a breeding site for rare species but lies on a favoured bird migration route through the Alps. Here you might see the marsh harrier, eagle owl, bittern and purple heron.

Ridges

In the wilder valleys, such as those to the north of Bergamo – Val Brembana and Val Seriana – particularly as you approach the Orobie Alps, to the northwest of Lake Garda approaching the Adamello, and in the pre-Alps north and west of Lake Maggiore, you may see marmots (though you are more likely to hear their high-pitched whistle) and chamois (not to be confused with feral goats), with red deer in the forests.

The birds of the open ridges include golden eagle, alpine chough, snowfinch and alpine accentor, while in

the forests are Tengmalm's owl, black woodpecker and the rare wryneck.

There is also a rich and varied plant life. The Grigna peaks to the east of Lake Como are famous for gentians. There is edelweiss here too, as well as Rainier's bellflower, which is restricted to the area and a few sites north of Bergamo.

Of all the ridge sites, the easiest to access, and one of the best in terms of scenery, is Monte Baldo on Lake Garda's eastern shore. Here there are several species of flower found nowhere else, as well as other, more common, alpine plants, together with eagles and other high mountain birds such as alpine chough, alpine swift, alpine accentor and snowfinches.

The BEST of

Five Great Viewpoints

From the **summit of Monte Baldo** above Malcésine (➤ 76–77 and 170–171).

From the **Church of Madonna di Monte Castello** on the Tignale plateau (➤ 57 and 177).

From the **summit of Monte Brione** above Riva del Garda (➤ 72).

From the **battlements of Sirmione's castle** (➤ 53 and 172–173).

From **San Rocco** (➤ 185).

Five Historical Sites

The fields of Solferino and San Martino della Battaglia, where the bloodiest battles of the Risorgimento were fought (➤ 78).

Sirmione, for the Roman remains and the Scaligeri Castle (➤ 53).

Lazise, for its old harbour and the Palazzo dei Capitano (➤ 79).

Lago di Ledro, for its extraordinary Bronze Age lake dwellings (➤ 56).

Limone sul Garda, for a last view of the lemons that once made the lake famous (➤ 56–57).

The Must See Top 10

Il Vittoriale, for its glorious mix of the fascinating and the kitsch (➤ 50–52).

The Heller Garden at Gardone Riviera, for the plant life (➤ 49).

Malcésine Castle, the emblem of the lake (➤ 76).

Salò Duomo, the finest church on the lake (➤ 46–48).

Sirmione, for its castle and Roman remains (➤ 53–55).

Desenzano del Garda's old harbour, for the beautiful blend of old and new (➤ 60).

Riva del Garda's lakeside, where town and water meet (➤ 70–72).

Monte Baldo's high ridge, for the ride in the cable-car, the view and the wild scenery (➤ 76).

Tremósine and Tignale, for the exquisite pastoral scenery, the peace and quiet (➤ 57).

Bardolino's wine *cantine*, to sample, to enjoy and to buy (➤ 79–80).

Finding Your Feet

First Two Hours

Arriving By Air

The northern Italian lakes are well served by air, with seven airports spread across the area, from Malpensa in the west (close to Lake Maggiore) to Venice in the east (which is just an hour's drive from Lake Garda).

Milan Linate Airport

- With Malpensa, Milan Linate is one of Milan's two main airports. It is **2km (1 mile)** from the eastern side of Milan's *autostrada* ring and 7km (4 miles) from the city centre (tel: 02 74851; www.sea-aeroportimilano.it).
- If you are **approaching the airport from the south** the exit is to your right (as usual), but if you are approaching from the north the exit is to your left, ie you exit from the fast lane. This catches many people unawares, especially as the signing is a little late.
- **Alitalia, British Airways and bmi baby** fly to Linate, as does **easyJet**, which has flights from London Gatwick and Heathrow airports.
- All major international and domestic **car-hire firms** are represented.
- If you are **driving to lakes Orta, Maggiore, Lugano or Como**, it is best to join the *autostrada* heading south (towards Bologna and Genoa), following the ring past the A1, A7 and A4 exits to join the A8 heading north. The A8 will take you to Varese, the A8/A26 to western Lake Maggiore and Lake Orta. Exit at Sesto Calende (Sesto C) to reach eastern Maggiore.
- For **Lugano and Como**, follow the A9 from the A8. To use the *autostrade* to enter Switzerland remember that a *carnet* is needed.
- If you are heading for **Bergamo, Bréscia, Verona or Lake Garda**, head north on the Milan ring *autostrada* and then follow the A4 towards Venice.
- If you are **travelling by train** from the airport you will need to get to Milan first. The easiest way to do this is on City Bus 73 – go out of the main exit and bear slightly left. You must buy your ticket before boarding the bus: they are available from kiosks inside the airport (€1). The bus terminates at San Babila after about 25 minutes. From here take the metro to Stazione Centrale.
- The **Star Fly bus** operates directly from the airport to Stazione Centrale. It leaves every 30 minutes and takes about the same time. The fare (€4) is payable on the bus.
- There are **taxi services** from the airport but they are expensive.

Milan Malpensa Airport

- Malpensa is situated close to Gallarate, to the south of Lake Maggiore. It is **6km (4 miles)** from the A8 *autostrada* and 50km (30 miles) from Milan city centre (tel: 02 74851; www.sea-aeroportimilano.it).
- All major international and domestic **car-hire firms** are represented.
- There is a **railway connection**, the Malpensa Express, between Terminal 1 and Milan's Stazione Cadorna. The journey takes about 45 minutes and costs €11 at the ticket office (€13 on board). Trains run every half-hour all day. From Terminal 2 there is also a bus, the Malpensa Shuttle Air Pullman, to the centre. It is cheaper (€6) but takes an hour. The bus leaves approximately every 15 minutes past the hour (times vary depending on the time of day).
- There are **shuttle buses** between Malpensa and Linate.

Bergamo Orio al Serio

- **Ryanair** flies to Orio al Serio from Luton and Stansted; **JET2** flies here from Belfast, Edinburgh and Manchester.
- The airport is **5km (3 miles)** southeast of the city and close to the A4 *autostrada* (tel: 035 320402; www.sacbo.it).
- All major international and domestic **car-hire firms** are represented.
- **Buses** run from outside the main arrivals exit to the main railway station in Bergamo. Tickets cost €1.65.
- There are also **buses to Bréscia and Milan**.

Bréscia Gabriele D'Annunzio

- **Ryanair** flies to Gabriele D'Annunzio from London Stansted.
- The airport is **20km (12 miles)** southeast of the city, near Montichiari (tel: 030 9656511; www.aeroportobrescia.it).
- All major international and domestic **car-hire firms** are represented.
- **Buses**, which connect with Ryanair flights, run from the airport (outside the main arrivals exit) to the city bus station (stop 24) and railway station. The buses take 30 minutes and cost €6. There are also buses to Verona's railway station. These take about an hour and cost €11 (€16 return). Tickets must be purchased inside the terminal.
- **Taxis** are available for a direct transfer to the city or to Desenzano del Garda. The latter cost about €35 and take about 35 minutes.

Verona Valerio Catullo at Villafranca

- **British Airways** flies to Villafranca from London Gatwick.
- The airport is **8km (5 miles)** northwest of the city (tel: 045 8095666; www.aeroportoverona.it). There is reasonable access to the A22 (and from it to the A4 *autostrada*).
- All major international and domestic **car-hire firms** are represented.
- **Buses** leave the airport every 20 minutes for Verona's Porta Nuovo railway station. The journey takes about 15 minutes and costs €4.50.
- **Taxis** to the railway station cost about €15.50 during the day, €18–€19 at night. They take about the same time as buses.

Treviso Ancillotto

- **Ryanair** flies to Treviso from London Stansted.
- The airport is **5km (3 miles)** west of the city (tel: 0422 315211; www.trevisoairport.it).
- Ryanair operates a **bus service** between the airport and Piazza Roma, Venice, costing €7. Each bus takes about 40 minutes.
- **Bus No 6** connects the airport to Treviso railway station and the city centre. It takes about 15 minutes and costs €1.50. From the railway station there are trains to Venice every 30 minutes from 5am to 11.45pm.
- Treviso will really only be useful to you if you are **hiring a car**. Follow the N13 south towards Venice to connect with the A4.

Venice Marco Polo

- Tel: 041 2606111, www.veniceairport.it
- **British Airways, bmi baby and easyJet** all fly to Marco Polo from London Heathrow, Manchester and Bristol; **JET2** flies here from Leeds and Manchester.
- Transport by **bus** and **waterbus** to Venice is well organised. If you are heading for the lakes your options are more limited. Buses run every 15 minutes to Mestre railway station, from where trains connect to points westward. The journey takes about 20 minutes and costs €3.

- All the major international and domestic **car-hire companies** are at Marco Polo.
- There is reasonable access to the **A4** *autostrada* from the airport.

Arriving By Road
- If you are arriving by road you will either cross the Brenner Pass from Innsbruck, following the A22 to northern Lake Garda and Verona, or cross the St Gotthard Pass from Lucerne to reach Lake Lugano and the A9 to Como, or cross the Simplon Pass from the Swiss Valais to reach Domodossola and lakes Orta and Maggiore.

Arriving By Train
- Trains, often night-sleepers, operate from all main European cities to both Milan and Venice and each city has connections to Verona and more local stations.

Arriving By Coach
- Eurolines operates long-distance coach services between 31 major European cities, including London, Frankfurt, Hamburg, Milan and Venice.

Tourist Information Offices

The main tourist offices are at:

Lombardy
Via Marconi 1, Milan (beside the Duomo)
Tel: 02 72524301, fax: 02 72524350
This is the main tourist office for Milan and the Lombardy region.

Via Gombito 13, Bergamo
Tel: 035 242226, fax: 035 242994

Piazza Loggia 6, Bréscia
Tel: 030 2400357, fax: 030 3773773

Piazza Cavour 17, Como
Tel: 031 330011, fax: 031 269712

Via Carobbio 2, Varese
Tel: 0332 283604, fax: 0332 283604

Piemonte
Corso Cavour 2, Novara
Tel: 0321 378443, fax: 0321 378458
For information on Lake Orta and western Lake Maggiore it is better to contact the tourist offices at Orta San Giulio and Stresa.

Trentino/Alto Adige
Via Manci 4, Trento
Tel: 0461 216000, fax: 0461 216060
Although this is the main office, for Lake Garda it is better to contact:
Piazza Garibaldi Giuseppe 7, Riva del Garda
Tel: 0464 554018, fax: 0464 520308

Veneto
Via degli Alpini 9 (southwest side of Piazza Bra), Verona
Tel: 045 8068680, fax: 045 8003638

All towns and most villages also have a tourist office dealing with their local areas. Most of these offices are open seasonally and so may have limited hours or be closed from November to March.
Remember that unlike most European countries, you do NOT drop the first 0 when dialling Italy from abroad from a land line.

Admission Prices
The cost of admission to the places of interest is indicated by the following price categories.
Inexpensive under €2 **Moderate** €2–€5 **Expensive** over €5

Getting Around

Bus Services
- There are buses along the **shore roads** of all the major lakes, and along the eastern shore of Lake Orta. The services are good, but infrequent on the smaller lakes.
- On **Lake Garda** bus 80 links Riva del Garda and Desenzano del Garda, while buses 62 and 64 link Riva del Garda and Verona.

Taxis
- Taxis are **expensive** and are not usually a first option for long journeys.
- They are **metered**, but it is worth asking what the final price will be before you get in.
- There are **taxi ranks** in all main towns and local companies post advertisements in hotels.

Rail
- **Fast and efficient** railways link the cities of the Lombardy Plain. From the cities, branch lines serve the eastern shore of Lake Orta; the western shore of Lake Maggiore as far as the Toce River; the eastern shore of Lake Maggiore all the way to Switzerland; the eastern shore of Lake Lecco/Lake Como; and the eastern shore of Lake Iseo.
- **Lake Lugano is poorly served**, as is Lake Garda, which has stations only at Desenzano and Peschiera.

Lake Steamers
- All six of the large lakes (Orta, Maggiore, Lugano, Como, Iseo and Garda), have **steamer services linking the main towns**. The summer and winter schedules vary (with fewer services in winter) so consult local timetables, which are posted at all steamer quays and are available in local tourist offices.
- As a general rule, there are **commuter services** to and from the main towns early in the morning and late in the afternoon.
- There are **two types of steamer**. The usual form is a diesel-engined ship that makes a slow journey around the lake. The faster hydrofoils (*aliscafo*) run less often and visit fewer places.

Ferries

- The **three large lakes** car ferries with services operate the following towns: Verbania and Laveno on Lake Maggiore; Menàggio, Varenna and Bellàgio on Lake Como; and Toscalano Maderno and Torri del Benaco on Lake Garda. The ferries **shuttle back and forth** across the lakes and run approximately every half-hour.
- The **cost depends on size of car and number of passengers**, but it is very reasonable compared with the time and cost of driving around.

Driving

- Italian roads are excellent. **Sections of the *autostrade*** are two-lane, which means they can become congested if slow-moving lorries form convoys.
- The **lake roads** are good, though care is needed in places, for instance the eastern shore of Lake Maggiore, the road from Como to Bellàgio and the parts of the eastern shore of Lake Garda where the roads are narrow.
- Look out for **local drivers** travelling at speed, and lane discipline, particularly in urban areas, can be poor.
- If you go into **Switzerland** and drive on their motorways (green signs) you must buy a Swiss motorway tax sticker. To avoid the motorways follow the blue signs to your destination.

Driving Essentials

- Drive on the **right-hand side** of the road.
- The wearing of **seat belts** in both the front and rear seats is obligatory.
- An appropriate harness system for **children aged 3–12** is obligatory.
- **Children under 4** must be in an appropriate child safety seat.
- **Children aged between 4 and 12** must travel in the rear seats.
- The use of **hand-held mobile telephones** while driving is prohibited.
- It is obligatory for **motorcyclists** to wear crash helmets.
- Car drivers must carry a **warning triangle and spare bulbs**, as well as a fluorescent waistcoat for use in emergencies.
- UK travellers must fit **headlamp deflectors**.
- **Dipped headlights** must be on at all times outside built-up areas.
- The **speed limit** on *autostrade* is 130kph (80mph). On main roads it is 110kph (68mph), on minor roads 90kph (56mph). In urban areas the limit is 50kph (30mph).
- There is random **breath testing**. The alcohol limit is 80 micrograms/100ml. Punishments are harsh.
- **Parking offences** in town attract an on-the-spot fine. You will not be allowed to move your vehicle until it is paid.
- Italian *autostrade* are **toll motorways**. Collect a ticket as you join and pay at the booths as you exit. Tolls can be paid in cash (sometimes by throwing coins into a catch net, but there is always an attendant) or by a card system. The latter is of limited value unless you are travelling a long way or using the motorways often.
- There are a good number of **service stations** on the motorways, varying from simple ones selling fuel and refreshments and with toilets, to grander buildings that include shops and high-class restaurants.

Bringing Your Own Car

To bring your own car you will need:

- A **valid driving licence** and the **original vehicle registration form**.
- A **green card** and original insurance cover note. Although in principle a green card is not needed as Italy is part of the EU, the Italian authorities require one to be carried.
- European **breakdown/recovery insurance**.

Accommodation

This guide recommends a cross-section of places to stay, ranging from inexpensive but comfortable hotels to those offering international standards of luxury. Standards of accommodation in Italy are generally very high and prices are comparable with those in other north European countries.

Booking a Hotel
- Booking ahead is recommended in high season.
- Travelling without pre-booking is easier in spring and autumn, but note that some hotels are open only during the summer season.
- Most tourist offices have lists of hotels, and a few offer a booking service for a small fee.

Italian Hotel Ratings
- The Italian classification of hotels is based on specific features rather than by overall standard. A swimming pool might make a three star into a four, while the absence of a pool might drop a four star to a three.

Rates
- The rate quoted will be for the room, not per person.
- Rates vary with season. Out of high season and late in the day it might be possible to negotiate a lower rate, but you should not assume this will be the case.
- Rates may or may not include breakfast. Check whether the quoted rate is *con colazione* (with breakfast), and if not how much breakfast costs and what it consists of. In larger, more expensive hotels the breakfast will be a buffet and almost certainly worth the money, but at some of the small, inexpensive hotels it might well be limited to bread, croissant and coffee. The local bar might offer the same meal for less money.
- In lakeside hotels there is usually a premium for lake-view rooms.

Rooms for Rent
- Rooms for rent are a popular form of accommodation, particularly in the Lake Garda area, where the sign *Zimmer* (rooms) is often seen.
- Renting a room for a night or two has great advantages if you wish to see behind the tourist veneer to a more genuine Italy. The families who rent rooms are usually extremely friendly and are often willing to cook dinner.

Camping
- Camping is popular in Italy but is not equally available on all the lakes.
- Lake Orta has no lakeside sites, though there are a few away from the lake near Orta San Giulio and Pettenasco.
- There is a limited number of campsites around Lake Maggiore, with good ones near Maccagno on the eastern shore and Baveno on the western shore. There are very few around Lake Como, and those that exist are away from the lake. There are also few around Lake Iseo. However, the eastern shore of Lake Garda is virtually one long campsite. The sites here vary from the good to the excellent and cater for everyone.

Prices: Expect to pay per double room, per night
€ under €70   €€ €70–€130   €€€ over €130

Food and Drink

Italian cooking is one of the great joys of travelling to the country. As a general rule, whatever grade of restaurant you choose the food will be both well cooked and well presented.

Specialities
- *Pasta*, of course, but also a surprising amount of rice dishes.
- Lake (freshwater) **fish**.
- **Meat specialities**, particularly in the mountain areas above the lakes, where rabbit and other game are popular.
- **Donkey** is also a speciality, particularly around Lake Orta and Mantova.
- **Local wines** include Barolo, Bardolino and Valpolicella.

Eating Places
The differences between the *pizzeria*, the *trattoria* and the *ristorante* are sometimes blurred.
- In general, *pizzerie* are inexpensive establishments serving various pizzas, some pasta dishes and may well have a salad bar too.
- *Trattorie* have a more extensive menu, but both the menu and the food will be 'no frills'. It will be well prepared and well served.
- *Ristoranti* tend to have the most extensive menus, with wider choices.

Tips
- Most restaurants add *pane e coperto* (bread and cover) to the bill.
- It is normal to **add a tip** as well as paying the *coperto*.

Eating Times
- The Italians eat a **light breakfast** between 7 and 9 in the morning.
- At **lunchtime** many shops close for an extended period to avoid working in the heat of the day. Lunches are leisurely and may last from 12 to 2.
- **Dinner** is the main meal of the day, eaten from 7pm onwards.

Drinks
- There is usually a **water jug** on the table, but it is becoming more frequent for diners to have to request mineral water with gas (*gastato* or *con gas*) or without (*naturale* or *senza gas*).
- **Wine** is usually drunk with lunch and dinner. Local wines are good value as the restaurant is likely to have a partnership with a local *cantina*.
- **Coffee** is usually served after the meal in various forms (➤ 17).

Bars
- If you want a coffee during the day try a **local bar**. Standing at the bar is known as *al banco* and prices are higher if you use the seats.
- In bars it is usual to pay for your drink first at the cash point. The cashier will give you a **purchase ticket**, which you then hand to the waiter behind the bar, who will make your drink.
- Bars are less expensive than **pavement cafés**.

Prices: Expect to pay for a three-course meal for one, excluding drinks and service

€ under €30   €€ €30–€60   €€€ over €60

Shopping

Italy is famous for its style and shopping in the cities and larger towns can leave you with a considerably smaller bank balance. Leather is an Italian speciality – shoes, handbags and jackets being of the highest quality. Lake Como – and particularly the cities of Como and Bellágio – are famous for their silk. Bardolino and Valpolicella in the east and Barolo in the west are famous wine-growing areas, and Lake Garda especially is famous for its olive oil.

Although there are few traditional crafts in the area, due to the cosmopolitan population, there are many artists' studios – painting, sculpture, ceramics, woodcraft and jewellery. There is also a number of excellent antiques shops.

Flea Markets
If you are searching for a bargain, the best are at:

Bréscia (Piazza della Vittoria) Held on the second Sunday of each month and excellent for antiques, furniture and objets d'art.

Como (Piazza San Fedele) Held on the first Saturday of each month and excellent for antiques and objets d'art.

Cremona (by the cathedral) Held on the third Sunday of each month and excellent for furniture and objets d'art.

Mantova (Piazza Castello) Held on the third Sunday of each month and excellent for antiques.

Varese (Piazza Montegrappa) Held on the first Sunday of each month and excellent for antiques and objets d'art.

Verona (Piazza San Zeno) Held on the first Sunday of each month and excellent for antiques, objets d'art and crafts.

Entertainment

Arts and Festivals
The lakes area has a huge programme of events each year, varying from the internationally famous – the Stresa Music Festival and the Verona opera season in the Arena – to more local events. The latter can be anything from a small music festival – jazz, rock, classical – to a regatta or folk dancing. The local tourist office will be able to supply details. Among the more interesting annual events are:

3–5 January
Canto della Stella – starlight singing in the villages of Tignale as the journey of the Magi is re-enacted with night-time processions.

February
Carnival season. The most famous is at Venice, but the *Gnoccho Bacchanalia* at Verona is excellent and there are good carnivals in other lake towns.

Lent
'Hag's trials' at Gargnano and Gardone. The effigy of an old woman is burnt in an echo of nastier times in medieval Italy.

Easter
Processions in the Swiss villages of Lake Lugano.

9–10 April
Bergamo pageant recalling the foundation of the Lombard League.

***c*24 June**
Sunday after St John the Baptist's Day. Boats process on Lake Como, followed by an open-air service on Isola Comacina. There are also rowing-boat races.

Summer
Various festivals – Verona's opera season, numerous music festivals, including that at Stresa. Also folklore festivals in the valleys around the lakes.

September
Grape Festival at Bardolino. *Palio del Baradello*, Como, with horse and boat races in medieval costume.

September/October
Festivals of traditional foods in the villages of Lake Maggiore.

Bars, Clubs and Discos
There are bars in all the lake villages, clubs in most of the towns and discos in some towns and all the cities. Some of the larger campsites on Lake Garda also have their own bars/discos.

Outdoor Activities
The lakes are, of course, superb for watersports – sailing and windsurfing chiefly, but also waterskiing and diving in some places. The high ridges that define the lakes are excellent walking country and the area also offers opportunities for more adventurous sports such as rock climbing. Horse-riding is also very popular and there are numerous opportunities for other outdoor sports, such as tennis and golf. For further details, ► 12–13.

Cultural Activities
Although the more southerly Italian cities – Florence, Siena, Rome, and not forgetting Venice – are more usually associated with the Renaissance, the northern city states also shared in the explosion of art and architecture that defined the period. There are, therefore, many museums, galleries and churches with treasure troves of artwork. Later, the climate of the area brought the rich, especially in winter, and many of the villas they built and the parkland they created are now open to the public.

Western Lake Garda

Getting Your Bearings

There are more towns and villages on the west side of Lake Garda than on the eastern side – and they are larger. This was the shore to which the villa builders came, despite the fact that here the terrace between the base of the confining ridge and the water's edge is narrower. So narrow, in fact, that on occasions the lakeside road – the Gardesana Occidentale – has had to burrow its way through the cliffs that plunge straight into the water.

The villas are one of the features of the western shore: Il Vittoriale, d'Annunzio's outrageous legacy; villas where Mussolini and his henchmen lived when, in 1944, their greed for power overcame common sense. Mussolini's last desperate effort was the formation of a republic within Italy, its capital at Salò. Today Salò has shaken off this infamous episode and is one of the most interesting towns on the western shore, its Duomo a masterpiece of Gothic architecture. Here, too, are Sirmione – strictly a southern shore town – the most

The harbour at Toscolano Maderno

The nave of Salò's Duomo

★ Don't Miss

picturesque place on the lake, Desenzano, with its marvellous old port, and Limone, where, it is said, the lemons that once made the lake famous were first grown.

But the western shore is not all town and villa. High above Limone and Gardone are the twin high plateaux of Tignale and Tremósine, where a pastoral peace replaces the bustle of the water's edge.

At Your Leisure

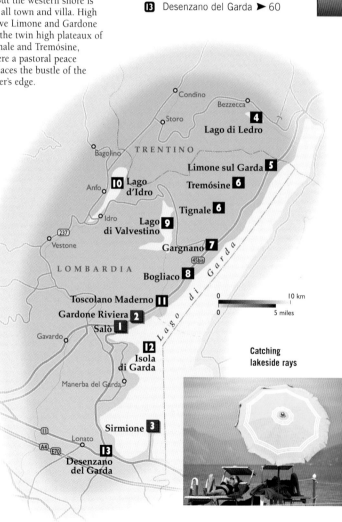

Catching lakeside rays

The drive along Garda's western shore first takes you up to the Tremósine and Tignale plateaux, then south past historic villas and towns.

Western Lake Garda in Two Days

Day One

Morning/Lunch

Make an early start from 5 **Limone sul Garda** (above, ► 56–57), heading south along the lakeside road for about 6km (4 miles) through four tunnels, then turn right to follow the road up on to 6 **Tremósine** and across to Tignale (► 57). Follow the drive (► 174–177) across the twin plateaux, visiting the Church of Madonna di Monte Castello (► 57) to enjoy the views and the artwork. Now descend past panoramic viewpoints of the lake and the eastern shore – particularly Malcésine and Monte Baldo – to reach the lakeside road again near 7 **Gargnano** (► 57–58). Have lunch at Gargnano, perhaps at Bar Azzurra, Piazza Zanardelli 9.

Afternoon

Head south along the lake road, stopping for a quick look at 11 **Toscolano Maderno** (► 59) before continuing to 2 **Gardone Riviera** and visiting Il Vittoriale (► 50–52).

Evening

Relax at one of the lakeside cafés in Gardone, then enjoy the cool of early evening and stroll along the lakeside promenade. Later, have a meal at the Trattoria da Marietta in Via Montecucco. Stay overnight in Gardone (► 61).

Day Two

Morning

Make another early start so you can beat the crowds into **1 Salò**
(➤ 46–48), where the parking can be a problem at the height of the
season. The main reason for the visit to is view the Duomo, but if you are
a music lover, and especially if your taste includes the violin, you will
want to visit the statue of Gasparo de Salò (➤ 25) at the town hall.

Late Morning/Lunch

It does not take long to
drive from Salò to
13 Desenzano (left, ➤ 60),
though the coastal road,
which offers continuous
views of the lake and
12 Isola di Garda (➤ 59–60),
takes longer. At Desenzano
have lunch at the old port,
or in nearby Piazza
Malvezzi, where Caffé Italia
at No 19 is very good.

Afternoon

Now head for **3 Sirmione**
(➤ 53–55), just a short
drive along the southern
shore. Explore the town by
following the walk
(➤ 172–173), which takes
in most of the historic sites,
but then spend time enjoying this most picturesque
lake town (below).

Evening

In the late afternoon choose one of the many options for a coffee and
watch the light play on the water. Then have a meal, perhaps at the
Trattoria La Fiasca in Via Santa Maria Maggiore, before a late evening
stroll to watch the sun go down. Sirmione is not only picturesque, but also
achingly romantic: watch the last of the sunlight licking the walls of the
castle, then head for your hotel.

Salò

Set in a long, narrow bay and backed by a ridge of high hills, Salò has a prime position on Lake Garda's western shore. The agreeable climate and advantageous site were not lost on the Romans, who founded a town they named *Salodium*. A thousand and more years later Salò was important enough to be the capital of the Magnifica Patria, the assembly of local towns formed in an attempt to bring some stability to an area at the border of the empires of Milan and Venice.

Several more centuries later the benign climate drew the rich and leisured, who built sumptuous villas – one of the reasons why Mussolini chose the town as the capital of his infamous republic (▶ panel opposite).

In 1901 an earthquake hit the area but much of the old town survived and what rebuilding there was enlarged and modernised the town, making it an ideal place both for a restful stay and as a centre for exploring the southwestern shore of the lake.

Above: Salò seen from Cisano

Left: street lamps in Salò represent Minoan sacral horns

Duomo

Among the maze of squares and narrow streets of the old town is the **Duomo**, one of the finest

The Salò Republic

By 1943 Italy's situation was desperate. The Allies had landed in Sicily, food was short and hope of victory had been replaced by fear of catastrophic defeat. Mussolini was forced to resign and Hitler ordered troops into Italy in a last effort to hold the country. On 13 October the new Italian government declared war on Germany, but by then Mussolini had been spirited out of Rome to Lake Garda, the Germans still holding the north of the country. The puppet Salò Republic was set up and Mussolini, the head of state, and his ministers were installed in local villas. The farce lasted a little over a year, Mussolini's grasp on reality loosening as 1945 approached. He told anyone who would listen that Germany had new weapons, and that Italian scientists had also invented terrible devices, and that these would surely win the war – pure fantasy on his part. Backed by the brave efforts of the Italian partisans, the Allies gradually occupied the whole of Italy. After a last meeting in Milan, Mussolini was finally forced to flee. With a German escort and wearing a German uniform he travelled up the western shore of Lake Como, but was intercepted and arrested, then executed the following day.

Mussolini (centre left) with his political ally, Hitler (centre right)

late-Gothic buildings on the lake. Inside is a towering combination of dark stone and brighter paintings. These paintings include works by Romanino and Zenon Veronese, and a golden polyptych by Paolo Veneziano.

In the square in front of the Duomo, Europe's finest orchestras hold summer concerts, a fitting reminder of the town's importance in the history of music (► 25).

Museums

Salò's **Museo Civico Archeologico** has items excavated from Roman *Salodium*, while the **Museo de Nastro Azzuro**, at Via Fantoni 49, covers the history of the Italian military from Napoleonic times to 1945. One room is devoted to the Salò Republic (► panel above).

Did You Know?

Nastro Azzuro means 'blue ribbon'. Although the colours of the Italian flag are red, green and white, Italy's national colour is blue: the national football team wears blue and is called the Azzuri, the Blues.

Piazza della
Vittoria in Salò

TAKING A BREAK

Salò's lakeside promenade has many cafés and restaurants, and there are more restaurants in the old town centre. Try **Bar Posta** at Via Canottieri 16.

➕ 200 B4
Museo Civico Archeologico
✉ Via Fantoni 49 ☎ 0365 296827 🕐 Tue–Fri 10–12 💶 Moderate

Museo Nastro Azzuro
✉ Via Fantoni 49 ☎ 0365 296827 🕐 Sat–Sun 10–12, 3–6 💶 Moderate

SALÒ: INSIDE INFO

Top tips Salò's **one-way system** is a nightmare if you are trying to park close to the Duomo. Instead, follow the signs for the city centre and the hospital to reach a car park close to the hospital. From here it is a short walk to Via Canottieri, where new bridges will take you quickly to the main promenade and in a few minutes you'll reach the old town and the Duomo.
• If you are **short of time** wander the old town and see the Duomo then have a coffee on the promenade.

Hidden gems Pasticceria Vassalli, at Via San Carlo 84/86, sells the best selection of chocolates on the western lake. After your visit, go to the town hall's first-floor council room to see the statue of **Gasparo de Salò** at work on a violin.

2 Gardone Riviera

In the late 19th century Ludovic Rohden, a German doctor and climatologist, visited the western shore of Lake Garda and was astonished by the benign nature of the climate. Not only were winters mild, but they were consistently so – offering an escape from snow and cold. Rohden extolled the virtues of the area and soon expensive villas graced the shore, the riviera, around the little town of Gardone. Even the Austrian Emperor himself was tempted, having the Villa Alba built in 1904, though he never managed to find the time to visit it.

Villa Alba and the Heller Garden

The villa, which stands behind the Torre San Marco, is now a conference centre. As well as villas hotels sprang up, one of the finest being the Grand, built in the 1880s by the German architect Ludwig Wimmer.

If your lakeside walk leads you to the lake steamer quay, cross into Piazza Marconi and follow Via Roma to reach the **Heller Garden** (Giardino Botanico) where more than 2,000 varieties of plants and flowers thrive, another tribute to Gardone's climate. The rock gardens were the work of Dr Arturo Hruska, who lived here from 1940 until his death in 1971; many authorities claim the gardens to be the finest of their kind in Italy, if not in Europe. Now taken over by poet, singer, writer, film-maker and artist

The classical portico of the Villa Alba

These decorated poles stand out against the trees in the Heller Garden

Right: Gabriele d'Annunzio's mausoleum, at Il Vittoriale

D'Annunzio's old Fiat Tipo, kept at Il Vittoriale

André Heller (born 1947), the gardens combine the horticultural interest of the founder with pieces of artwork that appeal to the present owner.

You can continue along Via Roma for about 350m (382 yards) to reach Il Vittoriale, but it can also be reached from Via Panoramica, which leaves the lake road at a point close to the Torre San Marco, a tower modified by Giancarlo Maroni, d'Annunzio's architect, to look more Venetian. D'Annunzio (► panel opposite) once kept his boats here.

Il Vittoriale degli Italiani

Villa Cargnacco, the villa transformed into Il Vittoriale, belonged to Henry Thade, a German art critic, until 1915 when it was confiscated by the Italian government, who sold it to d'Annunzio in 1921. With the help of the architect Giancarlo Maroni and his own eclectic collection of art and bric-à-brac, d'Annunzio converted the understated villa into what you see today. There is too much here to be able to describe it all in detail; beyond the entrance, to the left, is a replica of the bridge over the Pieve where the Italians halted the Axis advance in World War I, while to the right is the open-air theatre where d'Annunzio's plays are performed in summer. The view from the theatre takes in Lake Garda from

Sirmione to Monte Baldo. The Prioria (Priest's House) is crammed with objects, the bathroom alone having 2,000 items (as well as a bath). In a reception room a mirror sits below an inscription that d'Annunzio made Mussolini read when he visited – 'Remember, you are of glass and I of steel'.

D'Annunzio was eccentric; he hated daylight and had the windows painted black; wanted visitors to bow to him and had the door lintel to his study lowered so they would have to; and covered the bust of Eleanor Duse, one of his numerous lovers, to prevent the sight of her distracting him from his work. In the garden, the ship *Puglia* (the lower section replaced by concrete) recalls a famous incident at Fiume when her captain

Gabriele d'Annunzio (1863–1938)

Though born to modest parents, the self-styled Gabriel of the Annunciation grew up to be anything but a modest man. His poetry is now considered to be the epitome of the Decadent style. Now thought to be in poor taste, it was once the pride of Italian literature, arousing strong right-wing ideals. D'Annunzio was vocal in his enthusiasm for Italian participation in World War I and, many believe, was a prime reason for the country's involvement, despite its being woefully ill prepared for such a venture. In 1918 he famously headed a squadron of planes that flew over Vienna dropping anti-Empire/anti-war leaflets. When the peace did not bring the anticipated rewards for Italy in September 1919, d'Annunzio led a rebel army to capture Fiume (Rijeka), which he believed Italy deserved for its contribution to the war effort. The occupation caused embarrassment, but not until January 1921 did he retreat to Lake Garda. There he bought a villa that had been confiscated from a German in 1915 and had it transformed into a reflection of his own character – eccentric, flamboyant, grandiose; and they are the kinder words to describe him. D'Annunzio died in 1938 having already bequeathed his home to the Italian state, secure as he was of his place in history.

was wounded trying to rescue patriots. In hospital and bandaged, the captain took off the dressings against the doctor's wishes because he wanted to see the wounds: he promptly bled to death. D'Annunzio approved of the bravado and felt that Italy, too, should examine her wounds.

Finally there is d'Annunzio's tomb, his sarcophagus held aloft on square pillars and surrounded by the sarcophagi of heroes of Fiume.

TAKING A BREAK

It really should be somewhere close to the lake, perhaps the **Caffé Wimmer** in Piazza Wimmer opposite the lake steam quay. For a meal there are other opportunities in the town.

A view of the Grand Hotel

➕ 200 C4
Il Vittoriale
☎ 0365 296511 🕐 Park: Apr–Sep daily 8.30–8; Oct–Mar 9–5 (Sat and Sun 5.30). Villa: Apr–Sep Tue–Sun 9.30–7; Oct–Mar Tue–Sun 9–1, 2–5. War Museum: Apr–Sep Tue–Sun 9.30–7; Oct–Mar 9–1, 2–5 💰 Expensive

Heller Garden
☎ 336 410877 (cell phone) 🕐 Mid-Mar to mid-Oct daily 9–7 💰 Expensive

---

GARDONE RIVIERA: INSIDE INFO

Top tip At Il Vittoriale a **reduced priced entry ticket** is available that excludes the Prioria.
• To avoid the worst of the **queues** arrive very early, or at lunchtime.

Hidden gems Follow the **Barbarano stream** uphill from Gardone through little gorges with waterfalls and waterwheels, which drove an iron forge.

One to miss It's all down to personal taste of course, but the monumental, angular architecture of **d'Annunzio's mausoleum** is not worth the walk.

③ Sirmione

If you leave the A4 *autostrada* at the Sirmione/San Martino exit, or travel the road that follows the lake's southern shore, you will reach Colombare, a tidy if undistinguished village where a road heads off to Sirmione. This 4km (2-mile) drive starts straightforwardly enough, but soon the peninsula narrows dramatically so that it seems the lake has replaced the roadside verges. Shortly the road widens and reaches a car park (Sirmione is off-limits to all but essential vehicles so you have to leave your car here) and there, ahead of you, is one of the most magical places on the lake.

Entry to the town is by drawbridge and through the gate in the 13th-century walls built by the Scaligeri, lords of Verona. Though the Romans were here first, it was the Scaligeri who built the walls, the castle and the lake.

The Castle

The Rocca Scaligeri was built by Mastino I della Scala as a garrison and harbour for his galley fleet. Dante is reputed to have stayed here, and artists by the dozen have come to admire and draw inspiration: American poet Ezra Pound met Irish novelist James Joyce here – it would have been good to have been having a coffee on the next table when that happened.

Although the castle is now bare it is worth a visit (exterior only) for the view from the central tower that rises 29m (95ft) above the lake. Around the lake the Scaligeri

Entry to the town of Sirmione is through the 13th-century walls built by the Scaligeri, lords of Verona

fishtail battlements seen on the Rocco's walls and towers will become familiar. The site museum has stone tablets and galleys excavated from the Oglio River.

Old Town

Beyond the castle the town of Sirmione is crammed into about half the 70ha (173 acres) of the peninsula's head and comprises a maze of alleyways and streets with occasional views of the lake, olive trees or cypresses. To the right as you head away from the castle is the **Church of Santa Maria Maggiore**,

Catullus, the first love-poet

Catullus was born in 84BC in Verona and is claimed to have invented the love poem, his works dedicated to Lesbia, a married woman with whom he had an on-off affair. When she ended it, he is said to have died of a broken heart, at the age of 30. In one of his works he calls Sirmione the 'very eye of all peninsulas and isles that in our lakes of silver lie'.

built in the 15th century. The builders included a Roman capital in the porticoed façade.

Continuing through the town you will reach the **Catullo Spa**, the thermal water that first brought the Romans to the peninsula. Rising from beneath the lake at a temperature of 69°C (156°F), the sulphurous water is said to be excellent for the treatment of both muscular and sinus problems. Several hotels in the town also pipe the waters and offer thermal treatments to guests.

The Roman ruins at the Grotte di Catullo

Boat ride on the lake

Grotte di Catullo

At the peninsula's end are the Grotte di Catullo, named for the Roman poet Catullus (► panel above). The site is vast, the domestic buildings flanked by porticoes on each side and including a bath and swimming pool. Water is fed from the lake's thermal spring by lead piping. With its olive trees and marvellous views it would be good to believe that the love-torn Catullus really did live here, but though it is known he

had a villa at Sirmione, it is doubtful that he could have afforded so opulent a residence. An on-site museum displays the better finds from excavations here.

TAKING A BREAK

You really are spoilt for choice. The **Bar Al Cigni** at Vittorio Emanuele 12 is excellent, but the **Mancini G gelateria/bar** serves the best hot chocolate in town.

The beach at Sirmione caters for all kinds of activity

✚ 200 C2

Castello (Rocca Scaligeri)
☎ 030 916468 ◷ Tue–Sun 8.30–7 (exterior only) 💶 Moderate

Grotte di Catullo and Museo
☎ 030 916157 ◷ Mar–Oct Tue–Sun 8.30–7; Nov–Feb 8.30–5
💶 Moderate

SIRMIONE: INSIDE INFO

Top tip Sirmione can be **unpleasantly crowded at the height of summer**. Come before July or after September.
• The **Castello (Rocca Scaligeri)** and **Grotte di Catullo** are free to under 18s and over 65s.

Hidden gem Near the Catullo Spa is the **Church of San Pietro in Mavino**, begun in the 8th century on the site of a temple but rebuilt in about 1000. The church has some good Verona-school frescoes from the early medieval period.

At Your Leisure

4 Lago di Ledro

South of Riva del Garda a road branches right off the Gardesana Occidentale to reach Lake Ledro where, during construction work for a hydroelectric pipeline, Bronze Age dwellings were found. The Bronze Age dwellers drove wooden stakes into the lake bed and built their huts on the platforms they formed. When the level of the lake falls, up to 15,000 stakes may occasionally be revealed.

At Molina di Ledro, the village at the eastern end of the lake, a replica dwelling has been reconstructed. Here, too, there is a museum (**Museo delle Palafitte**), exploring the lifestyle of these lake folk.

Beyond Molina a road hugs the lake's northern shore: follow this, returning on a more winding road that stays close to the southern shore to return to Molina. At every point the views are superb.

Limone sul Garda's higgeldy-piggeldy terracotta-tiled rooftops

🚏 202 C3
Museo delle Palafitte
☎ 0464 508182 🕐 Jul–Aug daily 10–6; Mar–Jun and Sep–Nov Tue–Sun 9–1, 2–5 💰 Moderate

5 Limone sul Garda

Though the town was once famous for its lemons, its name in fact almost certainly derives from *limen*, meaning border – Limone having once been a border town between Italy and Austria. Lemons, and also citrons – a lemon-like fruit used in the production of *acqua di cedro*, a lemon brandy – and other citrus fruits were grown on terraces above the lake, the trees enclosed in green-houses during the winter to protect them from frost. With the unification of Italy, Sicily soon replaced Limone as chief producer of lemons and now little remains of the old terraces.

Until 1931 Limone was accessible only by boat and this isolation led to a remarkable evolution in the local people. The results of a study in 1979 showed that they had a protein in their blood called Apolipoprotein A-1 Milan gene Limone, which rids the arteries of fats and so virtually eliminates arteriosclerosis and heart disease. Not surprisingly, the discovery and its potential as a treatment has made Limone famous throughout the medical world.

The coming of the road ensured Sirmione's development as a tourist resort and although some of the subsequent development in the area has been unsympathetic, old Limone, with its arches, window boxes, balconies and shutters, is still delightful.

➕ 202 D2

6 Tremósine and Tignale

Between Limone and Gargnano, high above the lake, are the plateaux of Tremósine and Tignale, where flower-filled meadows, wooded slopes, rock faces, high hills and small villages combine to make one of the most beautiful areas on Lake

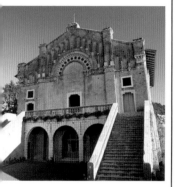

The Church of Madonna di Monte Castello, near Tignale

Garda. This is an area to explore on a leisurely drive (➤ 174–177) or even on foot, but if you have only a short time choose a day when the air is clear and take the road for Tignale, which leaves the Gardesana Occidentale to the north of Gargnano.

On this road there are belvederes from which to view the lake and Monte Baldo. A few kilometres farther on a short, steep road leads to the **Church of Madonna di Monte Castello**, built on the ruins of a Scaligeri castle and famed for its view and its artworks. The latter includes four paintings on copper attributed to Palma the Younger, and a fresco of

The Coronation of the Virgin, which some authorities claim is by Giotto.

➕ 202 C1
Church of Madonna di Monte Castello
☎ 0365 73019 🕒 Easter–Oct daily
9.30–7 💰 Free

7 Gargnano

Gargnano, home to the Centomiglia sailing event, held each September (➤ 64) and attracting boats from all over the world, is a lively little port. The Franciscans had a monastery here and it is claimed that it was at Gargnano that they grew Europe's

Colour-washed houses with arcaded loggias on Gargnano harbour

first lemon trees. The monastery church is still here, while the 13th-century cloisters are now a garden with lemon trees growing around the remains of the old stonework.

In 1866 Gargnano was an important town of the Magnifica Patria (➤ 46) and was bombarded from the lake by Austrian gunboats. The scars of this action can still be seen on the 16th-century Palazzo Comunale (the old town hall) near the port.

The neo-classical Palazzo Feltrinelli, overlooking the lake, was the seat of government of the Salò Republic; Mussolini lived in Villa Feltrinelli, which is now a study centre of Milan University.

✚ 201 D5
Church of San
Francesco and Garden
☎ 0365 71017 ⊙ Daily
8–8 ⬚ Free

8 Bogliaco

Tiny Bogliaco is famous
for having the best golf
course on the lake –
only 9 holes, but as
golfers will spend a
considerable time
gazing at the view, that
will be enough for an
afternoon – and for Villa
Bettoni Cazzago, second in size
only to the palazzo on Isola
di Garda.

**The grand villa on Isola di Garda was
built by the Borghese family**

The imposing 18th-century
building is surrounded by formal
gardens. It was the Headquarters of
the Council of Ministers of the
Republic. It is privately owned and
not open to the public but you can
admire the palazzo and the formal
Italian Renaissance garden from
the road.
✚ 201 D4

**Lago d'Idro, fed by the River Chiese, is one
of the highest Lombard lakes**

9 Lago di Valvestino

From Gargnano a road corkscrews
up and away from Lake Garda to
reach the Val Toscolano, in which
lies the mountain-shrouded Lago di
Valvestino, a man-made reservoir.
The valley heads north from the
lake's far end, climbing steeply to the
village of Magasa. This is excellent
walking country and many consider
the dramatic scenery to be just as
enticing as the more pastoral
Tremósine and Tignale plateaux.
✚ 200 C5

Bird and plant motif on the columns of the Basilica of Sant' Andrea

🔟 Lago d'Idro

Continuing westwards from Lago di Valvestino, or heading through the lovely Val Sabbia from Salò, you will reach the town of Idro, which shares its name with the little lake on which it stands. Idro is an enchantingly neat place with narrow streets and attractive old houses. There is also a church, San Michele, with fine wood-carving on the main altar, the organ case and the chorister seats in the choir. From Idro a road follows the eastern edge of the lake to reach the village of Vesta, where it ends. The views from here across to the castle at Anfo and the foothills of the Alps are superb.

On the western side of the lake the road burrows its way through the hills to reach Anfo, where the privately owned castle is another reminder of the Venetian republic. In 1866 the castle was the headquarters of Giuseppe Garibaldi during his campaign to add Veneto to the kingdom of Italy. The **Church of San Antonio** here has a 12th-century campanile and excellent Renaissance frescoes.

➕ 202 A1

🔟 Toscolano Maderno

Formerly two lake ports, but now combined into a single commune, Toscolano Maderno is considered by many to have the best beach on the lake, a title for which there is strong competition from resorts on the eastern shore. Maderno is the western terminus for Garda's car ferry (to Torri del Benaco). Its church, the Basilica of Sant' Andrea, is a fine 12th-century Romanesque building in which there is a masterpiece, *The Virgin and the Angel*, by Paolo Veneziano. The nearby Ionic column topped by the winged lion of St Mark is the only one now standing on Lake Garda. At the height of the Venetian Republic there would have been one in every lake village.

Legend has it that Toscolano was the first-ever lake settlement, the Etruscans arriving here in the 5th century BC. The Etruscan name for their port, Benaco, was also given to the lake, though later both the port and the lake changed name, the port taking the name of the leading local Roman family of Tuscolo.

One impressive feature of the twin towns is the **Orto Botanico Ghirardi**, a small garden begun in 1964. It has a collection of plants from across the world and includes greenhouses with tropical species.

➕ 200 C4
Orto Botanico Ghirardi
✉ Via Religione ☎ 0365 641246 or 02 50314863 🕑 May–Sep Wed and Fri 4.30–7 💰 Moderate

🔢 Isola di Garda

Isola di Garda is Lake Garda's largest island. It was once home to a monastery (which, legend has it, was visited by St Francis of Assisi), but that was abandoned and eventually became ruinous. In the 18th century the ruins – along with the rest of the island – were bought by the Borghese family, who constructed the largest, grandest villa on the lake. Shrouded in trees, the villa occupies one end of the island. The gardens and part of the villa are now open during summer months. Visits are guided and tie in with the ferry services. Entrance is included in the price of the ferry ticket.

On the mainland close to the island the area of olive- and vine-clad hills which fills the space from Salò to Desenzano is known as the Valtenesi, a region studded with old villages. At Padenghe, houses have been built within the old castle so that it looks like a hilltop village.

There is another, older, castle at Moniga del Garda, a village famous for Chiavetto, a rosé wine. At Manerba del Garda, the rocky headland, which offers fine views to Isola di Garda, is known as Dante's profile – not a complimentary comparison.

✚ 200 C3

◉ Ferries run Jun–Sep from various places around the lake to the island. For departure times, see www.isoladelgarda.com 🖫 Expensive

🔢 Desenzano del Garda

Desenzano is Lake Garda's largest town. It was founded by the Romans and the remains of a 3rd-century villa, the **Villa Romana**, have been excavated close to the harbour. The villa's mosaics are the finest in northern Italy and stand comparison with those of Pompeii. There is a site museum of excavated finds. Older finds from Desenzano's Bronze Age can be seen in the **Museo**

Archeologico Rambotti (Rambotti Archaeology Museum), housed in the cloisters of the Church of Santa Maria de Senioribus.

Today, Desenzano is a lively tourist centre, though the old port, with its trees and elegant buildings, is still the heart of the town. Streets of porticoed buildings lead off to either side, all lined with tempting shops and cafés.

Art lovers should seek out the **Church of Santa Maria Magdalene** in Via Roma, where there is a dramatic *Last Supper* by the Venetian artist Giovanni Battista Tiepolo (1696–1770), while those with more of an interest in technology could head for the lakeside memorial to the air speed record (709kph/490mph) set here in 1934 by Francesco Agello.

✚ 200 B2
Villa Romana
✉ Via Crocifiso 22 ☎ 030 9143547
◉ Tue–Fri 8.30–7 🖫 Moderate
(under 18s and over 65s free)

Museo Archeologico Rambotti
✉ Santa Maria de Senioribus, Via Anelli ☎ 030 9994275 ◉ Tue–Fri 3–7, Sat–Sun 2.30–7 🖫 Free

Lake steamers regularly come and go from Desenzano del Garda's harbour

Where to... Stay

Prices
Expect to pay per double room, per night
€ under €70   €€ €70–€130   €€€ over €130

DESENZANO DEL GARDA

Piroscafo €€
Adjacent to the old port. The rooms are simple but have air-conditioning and are well-maintained; some have balconies.

➕ 200 B2   ⊠ Via Porto Vecchio
📞 030 9141128/9140193;
www.hotelpiroscafo.it

GARDONE RIVIERA

Grand Hotel Gardone €€€
One of the lake's great hotels, with chandeliers, period furnishings and elegant bedrooms, plus a heated outdoor pool and private beach.

➕ 201 D5   ⊠ Via Repubblica 40
📞 0365 71128; www.hotelmeandro.it
🕓 Closed Nov–Mar

LIMONE SUL GARDA

Lido €€
Small and relatively inexpensive, the Lido is friendly and comfortable. All the rooms are pleasant, some with a lake view, and there is an excellent restaurant. Half board compulsory.

➕ 202 D2   ⊠ Via IV Novembre 34
📞 0365 954574/75; www.lidohotel.com
🕓 Closed Oct–Apr

SALÒ

Duomo €€€
A small hotel close to the lake with balconies overlooking the water, a sun terrace, indoor and outdoor Jacuzzis and a sauna.

➕ 200 B4   ⊠ Lungolago Zanardelli 91   📞 0365 21026;
www.hotelduomosalo.it

➕ 200 C4   ⊠ Corso Zanardelli 84
📞 0365 20261; www.grangardone.it
🕓 Closed mid-Oct to Mar

Monte Baldo €€
Inside has been refurbished and the bedrooms are well appointed. Meals are served on the lakeside terrace.

➕ 200 C4   ⊠ Via Zanardelli
📞 0365 20951;
www.hotelmontebaldo.it
🕓 Closed mid-Oct to Mar

GARGNANO

Meandro €€
Set in beautiful grounds near the lake. Good bedrooms.

SIRMIONE

Catullo €€
Lakeside position at the heart of the old town. A mix of old and modern furnishings, and large bedrooms, plus a sun lounge and gardens.

➕ 200 C2   ⊠ Piazza Flaminia 7
📞 030 9905811; www.hotelcatullo.it
🕓 Closed Jan–Mar

Sirmione €€€
A thermal hotel with the castle on one side and the lake on the other.

➕ 200 C2   ⊠ Piazza Castello 19
📞 030 916331; www.terme-disirmione.com

TREMÓSINE

Village Hotel Lucia €€
A hotel and holiday 'village' on the edge of the Tremósine. Views, sports facilities and a pool.

➕ 202 C1   ⊠ Via del Sole 2
📞 0365 953088; www.hotellucia.it
🕓 Closed mid-Oct to Mar

Where to...
Eat and Drink

Prices
Expect to pay for a three-course meal for one, excluding drinks and service
€ under €30   €€ €30–€60   €€€ over €60

DESENZANO DEL GARDA

Ristorante Pizzeria Kapperi €
A modern and spacious restaurant-cum-pizzeria, owned by a young team. Freshly made pasta dishes are a speciality. Good pizzas too.
🚹 200 B2 ☒ Via N. Sauro 7
☎ 030 9991893 🕒 Closed Mon pm

GARDONE RIVIERA

Trattoria da Moarietta €€
A short walk from Il Vittoriale, this is an unpretentious and friendly place. Simple menu with excellent food and a good wine list.
🚹 200 C4 ☒ Via Montecucco 78
☎ 0365 20960 🕒 Closed Thu

Villa Fiodaliso €€€
A meal here is one of the great dining experiences of the western lake. The restaurant is housed in a lavish villa (once the home of Claretta Petacci, Mussolini's mistress, who was executed with him in 1945), where a few rooms are also available. The menu chiefly comprises traditional dishes, and

offers a simple menu with well-prepared food and friendly service.
🚹 200 B4 ☒ Via di Mezzo 10
☎ 0365 290966 🕒 Closed Tue

SIRMIONE

Locanda La Noce €
Tucked between Jacky Bar and the Hotel Sole, this is a delightful *spaghetteria* with a terrace giving lovely views across the lake.
🚹 200 C2 ☒ Via Monsignor Comboni 33 ☎ 0365 954022
🕒 Closed Wed, Nov–Jan

Trattoria La Fiasca €
You'll find this charming restaurant up a side street in Sirmione. The minestrone soup is as thick as a stew and just as filling. The menu is uncomplicated, and the food is well cooked.
🚹 200 C2 ☒ Via Santa Maria Maggiore 1 ☎ 030 9906111
🕒 Closed Wed and Feb

the cooking, service and wine list are first-class. Booking is essential.
🚹 200 C4 ☒ Corso Zanardelli 150
☎ 0365 20158 🕒 Closed Mon and Tue lunch, and mid-Nov to Mar

PIEVE DI TREMÓSINE

Miralago €€
Possibly the best-positioned restaurant on Lake Garda, on the top of the cliff in Pieve di Tremósine. On a clear day the view is sensational. Straightforward cooking excellently presented. Some dishes include local chestnuts and mushrooms, each of which should be tried.
🚹 202 C1 ☒ Piazza Cozzaglio 2
☎ 0365 953001/953046 🕒 Closed Thu and mid-Dec to mid-Jan

SALÒ

Osteria di Mezzo €€
In a road that runs parallel to the promenade, two streets back from the town hall, this little restaurant

Where to... Shop

Most of western Lake Garda's towns are small, with limited shopping potential except Salò and Desenzano del Garda. The centres are mostly given over to cafés, restaurants, souvenir shops and a few more conventional outlets.

DESENZANO DEL GARDA

Cashmere Ironia (Via Porto Vecchio) sells tempting sweaters and scarves of its own production, while **Intimamente** (Via Santa Maria) has designer underclothes for men and women.

For jewellery go to **Giorelleria**, while try **Martinetti** (Via General Achille Papa 40) particularly for handbags and belts, and **La Bagagerie**,

(Via Porto Vecchio 22).

If you looking for art try **Galleria La Cornice** (Piazza Giuseppe Malvezzi 45) which has interesting modern artworks in wood, metal and ceramics, and paintings on wood.

GARDONE RIVIERA

Enoteca Bedussi (Corso Repubblica 40) sells a large collection of wines, spirits and local liqueurs, while **Antique Marino** (Piazza Marconi 6) has a good range of antiques – an unusual find in such a small town.

LIMONE SUL GARDA

There is a limited number of shops in the town, the best of which are **Pace Mirella** (Lungolago Marconi 14) for a huge range of dried fruits and nuts; and **Raffi**, on the same street, which sells designer clothes such as Armani and Valentino.

SALÒ

For handbags and elegant jewellery try **Tranquilli** (Via San Carlo 58); and for shoes try **Principe** (Lungolago Zanardelli 21a/22).

For a superb range of silverware, including goblets and bracelets, try **GB Argento** (Via Fantoni 10); **Quartiere Chic** (Via Fantoni 1) with kitchenware and linens for the home; and **Ottica Scotti** (Piazza G Zanardelli 7), for items in gold, silver and crystal.

The best antiques are at **Negozio d'Arte da Marinella** (Lungolago Zanardelli 29/30) while **Colorificio Nastuzzo** (Via Fantoni 35) sells artists' materials and offers courses in watercolour painting.

SIRMIONE

Via Vittorio Emanuele, linking the castle with the Catullo Thermal establishment (and a few of the side streets), has several fashion shops. Other outlets include **Cose Dal**

Mondo (Via Dante 15) for Asian antiques; **Art Gallery Donavil** (Via Dante 5) for Chinese antiques, English silverware and Murano glass; **l'Enoteca** (Corte Salvelli 6) and **Enoteca Il Volto** (Via Piana 16) which both have vast collections of wines; **Sogni Profumati** (Piazza Castello 12) where there is an amazing collection of soaps, candles and perfumes; and **Gioielli**, (Via Vittoria Emanuele 54) for jewellery, particularly amber.

MARKETS

There are good general markets at **Desenzano del Garda** – first and third Tuesday of each month; **Limone sul Garda** – first and third Tuesday of each month; **Manerba del Garda** – Tuesday; **Salò** – Saturday; **Sirmione** – Friday; **Toscolano Maderno** – Thursday.

There is also an excellent antiques market in Desenzano del Garda on the first Sunday of the month (except Jan and Aug).

Where to...
Be Entertained

SPORT AND LEISURE

Watersports

Sailing and **windsurfing schools** can be found at virtually every town and village on the lakes, and ad hoc schools also occasionally appear on the beaches.

There are good schools at Sirmione (**Martini**, tel: 320 1112465 and **Lana**, tel: 338 6243650 are among the best), Desenzano (**Fraglia Vela**, tel: 030 9143343) and Campione del Garda (**Vela Club**, tel: 0365 916908).

At the northern end of the lake there is a huge choice at Riva del Garda and Torbole (▶ 86).

The **Centomiglia Sailing Competition**, held at Gargnano in September, is one of Europe's premier events and attracts entries from far and wide.

Diving is good at the southern end of the lake and there are several schools at Desenzano, including **Asso Sub Il Pelicano** (tel: 030 9144449).

Boat hire is available in most of the lake towns.

Adventure Sports

The walking on Tremósine-Tignale is wonderful, and the plateaux also offer more adventurous opportunities with **parasailing** and **canyoning** and some excellent mountain bike trails. Details of clubs and venues can be obtained from the tourist office in Pieve (▶ 175).

Golf

There are few courses on the western shore. The **Club Palazzo Arzaga** (tel: 030 6806266) near Padenghe (just north of Desenzano) has 18-hole and 9-hole courses.

Close by, at Soiano del Lago there are 18-hole and 9-hole courses at the **GardaGolf Country Club** (tel: 0365 674707). There is also a 9-hole course at **Bogliaco** (tel: 0365 643006).

SPAS

Sirmione has many opportunities for relaxation, not only in its hotels but also at the **Catullo Thermal establishment** at Via Puntastaffalo 1 (tel: 030 916044).

FESTIVALS

The **Estate Musicoli Gasparado Salò** is a classical music festival held from July to September with open-air concerts in Piazza Duomo. Other concerts from July to September are held in Gardone Riviera, Desenzano del Garda and Gargnano. Classical music concerts are also held in Salò's **Palazzo Fantoni** in May and June and an **International Classical Music Festival** takes place in August in Manerba.

A **Guitar Festival** is held each September in Gargnano and a **Jazz Festival** from June to September at Gardone Riviera.

NIGHTLIFE

During the summer there is **open-air cinema and theatre** in Desenzano in the Castello. Around Desenzano is also the best area for discos and music bars. Of the current crop of discos, the best are **Sesto Senso** (tel: 030 9142684) at 67 Via dal Molin and **Art Club** (tel: 030 9991004) at la Via Mantova in Desenzano itself, **Dehor** in Via Mantova (tel: 030 9919955/9919948) and **Fura** (tel: 030 9130652) at 13 Via Lavagnone at Lonato.

Eastern Lake Garda

Getting Your Bearings

At first glance it might be said that the western shore of Lake Garda, with its villas, gardens and historic towns, is more for the lover of history and culture, whereas the eastern shore, with its beaches and campsites, appeals more to the sun-lover and the active visitor. There is an element of truth in that, but it is also an over-simplification.

At the southeastern tip of Lake Garda are the classic entertainment sites of Gardaland and the nearby waterparks. But this is also a land of vines, the famous wines of Bardolino being pressed from grapes grown within sight of the lake. Farther inland are the vineyards that produce Valpolicella, one of the great wines of Italy. There is history here too. At Peschiera the Austrians built huge fortifications to maintain their grip on this part of the country. The battle at Solferino loosened the Austrians' hold, but the legacy of massive walls remains.

The strategic importance of the lake is also reflected in the castles that pre-date Austrian Peschiera – Scaligeri castles with their familiar fish-tail battlements. Lazise is a fine example, but the best is at Malcésine, its tower having become a symbol of the lake. Between the two is Garda, the town which shares its name with the lake, while beyond Malcésine, at the head of the lake, is Riva del Garda, now an important tourist town but with a castle that hints at a less peaceful past. So history finds a place on the eastern shore, and if the east cannot match the profusion of villas on the west, it has its natural delights – Monte Baldo, above Malcésine, is one of the best and most accessible mountain ridges on the lake.

Outdoor socialising Malcésine style

★ Don't Miss

1. **Riva del Garda** ➤ 70
2. **Garda** ➤ 73
3. **Malcésine and Monte Baldo** ➤ 75

At Your Leisure

4. San Martino della Battaglia and Solferino ➤ 78
5. Parco Giardino Sigurta ➤ 78
6. Peschiera del Garda ➤ 78
7. Gardaland ➤ 79
8. Lazise ➤ 79
9. Bardolino ➤ 79
10. Punta di San Vigilio ➤ 80
11. Torri del Benaco ➤ 80
12. Torbole ➤ 81
13. Arco ➤ 82

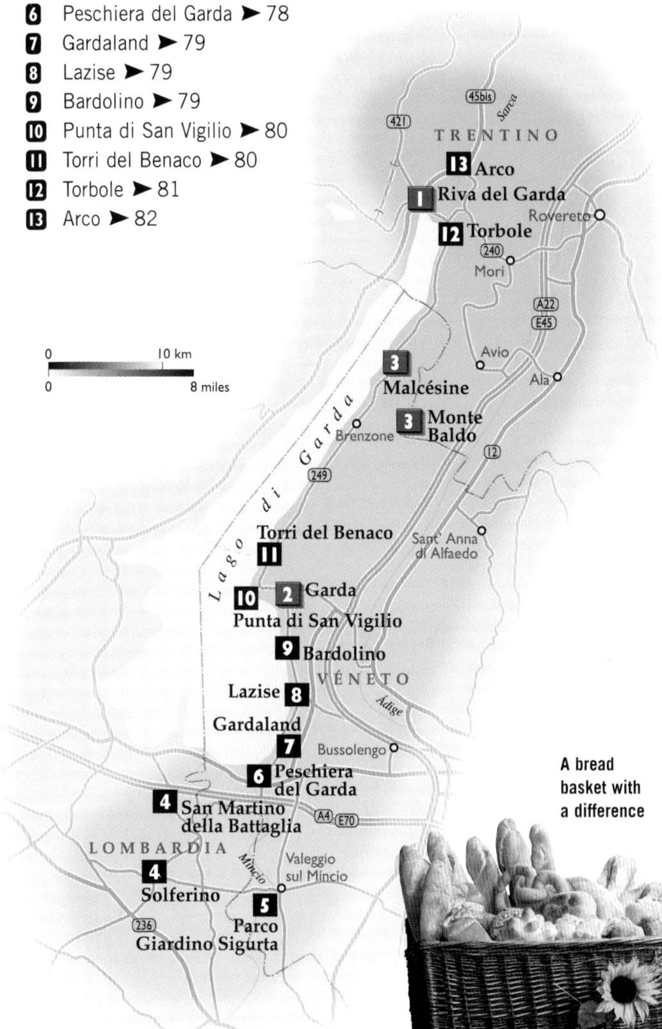

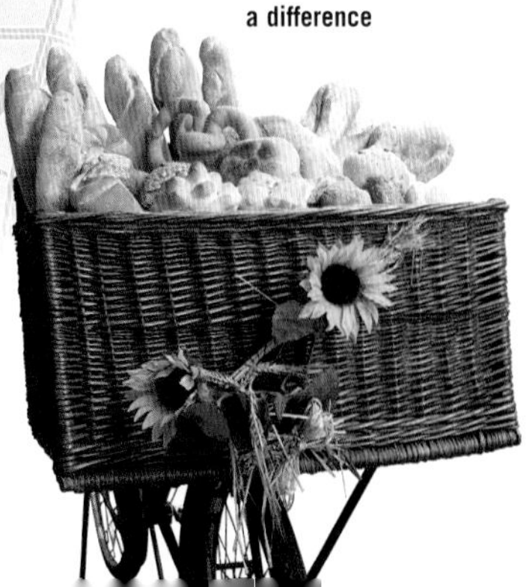

A bread basket with a difference

Travel up the eastern shore of the lake to Riva, with views
of the water all the way and vineyards, olive groves and
Scaligari castles to divert you.

Eastern Lake Garda In Two Days

Day One

Morning

Start the morning with a walk around the massive fortifications of
6 Peschiera del Garda (➤ 78–79), then take the lakeside road north to
8 Lazise (➤ 79). Here the old port, with its memories of the Venetian
Republic, and the still impressive Scaligeri castle are further reminders
of the importance of Lake Garda in medieval Italy. Have lunch at one
of Lazise's harbour restaurants – perhaps Alla Grotta, which has
fine views of the old port.

Afternoon

Continue north to **9 Bardolino** (➤ 79–80), whose vineyards have made the
town's name famous. You can visit the wine museum, which is also a
cantina, or take a short detour along part of the wine route that leads
through the vineyards past many of the finest *cantine*. Later, continue
north from Bardolino to reach **2 Garda** (below, ➤ 73–74).

Evening

After a stop for coffee and a short exploration of the town, drive about 4km (3 miles) to **10 Punta di San Vigilio** (➤ 80) to enjoy a swim at one of the most picturesque beaches on the eastern shore. Return to Garda for your evening meal – try the Casa Lady in Via Verdi – and then stay overnight in Garda.

Day Two

Morning/Lunch

You could head back to Punta di San Vigilio for an early swim to set you up for the day. Next travel north to **11 Torri del Benaco** (➤ 80–81), where there is another Scaligeri castle, this one housing a museum that will give you an insight into local olive oil production: you will soon be passing olive plantations on the flanks of Monte Baldo. Continue to Malcésine, but do not go into the town. Instead, head for the bottom station of the cable-car and take the short ride to the mountain-top café for a light lunch.

Early Afternoon

If time permits, walk along the high ridge (➤ 170) from the café, then take the cable-car to descend to **3 Malcésine** (left, ➤ 75–77) and explore the town's narrow streets and castle.

Late Afternoon

From Mascéline continue north beside the lake, enjoying the views across the water to your left and of the flanks of **3 Monte Baldo** (➤ 76–77) to your right. Continue around Monte Brione to reach **1 Riva del Garda** (below, ➤ 70–72).

Evening

The view of the lake from Monte Brione is exceptional so the short drive to the top is worthwhile. Or you could perhaps head north on the road to Trento for 6km (4 miles) to reach **13 Arco** (➤ 82). Alternatively, if exertions on Monte Baldo have left you short of time or energy, just enjoy Riva's lakefront before having a meal at one of the numerous excellent restaurants in the town (➤ 84).

❶ Riva del Garda

If you approach Riva from the south, along the eastern shore, the town is hidden by the wedge of Monte Brione until the road has crossed the Sarca River and burrowed its way through the rock. Positioned at the extreme northern tip of the lake, Riva has always been important as a trading centre.

At first the Bishops of Trento held the port, but the town was coveted by Milan, Venice and Verona, who each held it for periods during the 14th and 15th centuries. Its strategic value is reflected in the number and quality of its fortifications, civic buildings and houses, though the latter had to be extensively rebuilt when the town was destroyed during the War of the Spanish Succession in 1703.

Torre Apponale, Riva's clock tower, in the Piazza Tre Novembre

The Rocca

The Rocca, the town's moated castle, stands in Piazza Cesare Battisti, a step away from the main square, and is reached by a double-arched bridge and drawbridge. Verona's Scaligeri built it in the 12th century as much to defend the town from lake

pirates as to proclaim their ownership. Successive new lords of Riva later remodelled it, all wishing to make their mark on the town.

Today the castle houses the town library and **Civico Museo**, a concert hall and exhibitions of paintings. The museum includes items from the Lake Ledro Bronze Age dwellings (➤ 56), as well as some Roman items and medieval paintings and frescoes from local buildings.

The Old Town

The 13th-century **Torre Apponale** in the main square, Piazza Tre Novembre, which overlooks the harbour, has been in turn a fortified lookout tower, a grain store and a clock tower. It now offers a great view of the town. Also in the square are the 14th-century Venetian **Palazzo Pretorio** and the 15th-century **Palazzo Communale**, linked by porticoes and arches. Elsewhere in

Cascata del Varone

From Riva take the 421 – towards Lago di Tenno – for 4km (2 miles) to reach Varone, where a waterfall drops 90m (294ft) into a tight gorge. Walkways have been constructed to allow you to get close to the falls and admire their power and to experience the noise and spray. Warm and waterproof clothing is recommended.
☎ 0464 521421 ⓣ May–Aug daily 9–7; Apr and Sep 9–6; Mar and Oct 9–5; Nov–Feb Sun and public holidays only 10–5 💰 Moderate

the town the remnants of medieval walls and three wall towers have been incorporated into later buildings.

TAKING A BREAK

Riva has one of the most interesting lakesides of any of Lake Garda's towns. Choose a café or restaurant in Piazza Tre Novembre to get the best from it. **Caffé Città** is very good. There are also good places in town for a quiet coffee – try the **Maroni pasticerria** on the corner of Via Maria and Piazza Cavour.

➕ 202 D3
Torre Apponale
☎ 0464 573869 ⓣ Apr–Oct Tue–Sun 10–6. Also Mon in Jul and Aug 💰 Inexpensive

Civico Museo
☎ 0464 573869 ⓣ Tue–Sun 10–6, Apr–Oct. Also Mon in Jul and Aug 💰 Moderate

Monte Brione provides a dramatic backdrop to Riva

RIVA DEL GARDA: INSIDE INFO

Top tip Next to Piazza Tre Novembre there is an even prettier square – **Piazza San Rocco**, named after the church beyond it.
• For an excellent view of the town and lake take the winding road to the **bastione**, a 16th-century round tower built by the Venetians above the lake's western shore, south of the town.
• Another worthwhile excursion from the town is the drive to the top of **Monte Brione**, hairpin bends notwithstanding.

Hidden gem The best of the town's churches is the **Inviolate** on Via Roma (this is the road to Arco: the church is beyond the old, fortified San Michele city gate). Built in the early 17th century by an unknown Portuguese architect, it has an elaborate baroque, octagonal interior – all gilding and plasterwork.

One to miss If you are particularly interested in **lake dwellings**, go the museum at Lake Ledro (➤ 56) rather than the one here in the Rocca.

2 Garda

As you drive north from Peschiera, following the lakeside road, which hugs the water's edge, the huge rocky outcrop that dominates the town of Garda soon comes into view.

Looking across the lake towards Garda, which gave the lake its name

The Roman Empire famously fell to the 'barbarians at the gate', tribes with names now synonyms for the atrocious – Huns and Vandals. But there was another tribe, the Longobards or Lombards. They may have been considered barbarians by the Romans, and they were certainly pagan, but the Lombards were actually a sophisticated people with many modern ideas on social welfare and banking: it is no coincidence that London's bankers occupy Lombard Street. The Lombards built a fortress on the prominent outcrop near the lake's southern shore. Their word for a castle or defended lookout was *warte*, which, corrupted by 1,200 years of usage, is the origin of Garda.

Monte Garda

In the 10th century the castle on Monte Garda, as the outcrop is now called, was the most important on the lake. It was controlled by Berengar II, King of Piemonte, who had over-run the area in 960, killing Lothar, the local king. To complete his takeover Berengar decided to marry Lothar's widow, Adelheid, but so vehemently did she decline his offer that Berengar, a ruthless tyrant, had her imprisoned on Monte

Garda – presumably thinking that a few months of deprivation would change her mind. But Adelheid was resourceful and with the help of a trusted servant had a message taken to Otto the German Emperor, imploring his help. Otto brought an army south, defeated Berengar and married the grateful Adelheid. Having acquired northern Italy, Otto was crowned head of the Holy Roman Empire.

The pretty streets of Garda's old town just have to be explored

The Town

Equally important in the history of Italy was the treaty for the annexation of Lombardy to Piemonte in 1848, which was signed at Garda in the romantic, castle-like Villa Albertine. This was the major act of the First War of Independence, the initial attempt to unify Italy and to shake off Austrian dominance of much of the north. It was a further 10 years before the battles led to the fulfilment of the dreams of the Risorgimento.

Another poignant reminder of conflict lies 3km (2 miles) east of Garda at **Costermano**, where there is a German war cemetery with the graves of more than 20,000 soldiers from World War II.

Of the many fine villas in the town, one of the most interesting is the **Palazzo dei Capitani** in Piazza Catullo, close to the lake. The palazzo, architecturally plain apart from its arches and sculpted Gothic windows, housed the Venetian Empire's Captain of the Lake, who exercised the Doge's power.

The old town itself is exquisite. Now an important eastern shore resort, Garda has absorbed the development well, mixing the old and new in fine style. It is also an excellent centre for touring, the delights of **Gardaland** (► 79) and the other activity parks being just a short distance away.

Mending the fishing nets

TAKING A BREAK

Perhaps the **Bar da Franco** on the lake front for a coffee or the **Trattoria Bella Venezia** at Vicolo del Pio 12.

➕ 201 D3

GARDA: INSIDE INFO

Top tips Walk off a good lunch or work up an appetite for dinner by taking the 45-minute **walk to the top of Monte Garda**. Watching the sun go down from there is superb, and the path down is straightforward by twilight. Or stroll to **Punta di San Vigilio** and watch the world go by (► 80).

• There is a **good market** in the old town each Friday.

Hidden gem The **Church of Santa Maria Maggiore**, in Piazzale Roma, close to the old town, has a beautiful 15th-century cloister.

③ Malcésine and Monte Baldo

North of Peschiera del Garda the Gardesana Orientale, as the road beside the lake is called, runs through the Riviera degli Olivi (Olive Riviera). In its early stages the road passes more vines than olive trees, but farther north the silvery leaves of the trees shimmer on the hillside, seemingly mirroring the light bouncing off the waves on the lake. Beyond Cassone is the Val di Sogno (Valley of Dreams), which is as peaceful as its name. Offshore here are two small islands, Isola Sogno and Isola dell'Olivo (the islands of dreams and olives), while ahead is Malcésine, the highlight of the eastern side of the lake.

Malcésine's castle, former fortresss and now home to two museums

Malcésine

Scaligeri Castle dominates the town, though much of the fortress is difficult to see unless you are on a lake steamer. From the lake the genius of the construction is visible – a series of fortified walls surrounding three courtyards tumbling down a rugged headland. The castle was built by the Veronese on an original Lombard fortress in the 13th century, but was restored by the Venetians in the 17th century. Not only does it offer tremendous views, but it houses two small museums. One, the Parini, is devoted to the German dramatist and poet Johann Wolfgang von Goethe (1749–1832) and includes sketches he made during his Italian trip, while the other deals with local wildlife and prehistoric rock etchings.

Outside the castle, Malcésine is a tangle of narrow streets, some of them arcaded. Make your way to the lake to find the 15th-century Palazzo dei Capitani, the seat of the Veronese governor of the lake. The palazzo, a handsome building with pillars and arcaded windows, is now the town hall and houses a library named after Goethe (open to the public). From it there is a lovely view to the Island of Olives.

Monte Baldo

From Malcésine a cable-car will take you to the top of Monte Baldo, either to enjoy the view or for a walk along the high ridge (▶ 170). The flank of the great peak overlooking the lake is often known as the Botanical Garden of Italy because of the variety and profusion of plant species. Two parks have been set up to protect the plant life and the wildlife. The Lostoni Selva Pizzi has one boundary, which follows the crest of Monte Baldo's high ridge, the lower boundary running above the lakeside road. The second park, which shares its name with the road – Gardesana Orientale – is at the base of the hill between Malcésine and Torbole.

The change in vegetation visible from the cable-car is marked. Close to the lake there are olive groves together with holm oak and Mediterranean pine. Higher up there are alpine species such as gentians, alpine orchids (including black vanilla, small white, toothed and spurred fragrant) and such plants as *Lilium bulbiferum* and *Cyclamen purpurascens* or orange lily and sowbread, while at the top of the ridge the

The view from the top of Monte Baldo

species are those that would be expected on Arctic tundra rather than sun-soaked southern Europe – saxifrages and mountain avens, for example. As well as plants familiar from other European sites, Monte Baldo has three endemic plants, an anemone (*Anemone baldensis*), a bedstraw (*Galium baldensis*) and a speedwell (*Veronica bonorata*).

North of Malcésine, the builders of the Gardesana Orientale had so little room between the lake and the mountainside that they had to resort to tunnelling. The shorter of the two tunnels crosses the border between Veneto and Trentino.

TAKING A BREAK

In town the **Caffé al Porto**, near the harbour, and the **Caffé del Borso**, at Corso Garibaldi 8, are excellent, the latter selling the best hot chocolate in Malcésine.

Malcésine ➕ 202 D1
Monte Baldo ➕ 201 F5

Museo Castello Scaligeri
☎ 045 6570333 ◷ Apr–Oct daily 9.30–7 💰 Moderate

Cable-car to Monte Baldo
◷ Summer daily 8–7; winter 8–4. Cars run every 30 minutes; journey about 10 minutes. The cable-car is usually closed in Nov and early Dec for maintenance work
💰 Expensive

MALCÉSINE AND MONTE BALDO: INSIDE INFO

Top tip With the museum, bust and library it is difficult to escape Goethe; to complete the set search out the **plaque** to the poet's visit to the town.

One to miss If you are planning to visit **Capo di Ponte** (➤ 124), you can afford to skip the rock engravings in the castle museums.

At Your Leisure

❹ San Martino della Battaglia and Solferino

The two battles fought to the south of Sirmione (► 8–10) were instrumental in the creation of the Italian state and led to the establishment of the Red Cross (► 22, Henri Dunant). But the human cost was considerable. At San Martino an ossuary houses the bones of 2,600 soldiers who died. The 64m (213ft) Torre Monumentale at the summit of the nearby hill commemorates both the battle and the Risorgimento, while the museum behind it has mementoes of the conflict.

About 11km (7 miles) farther south, at Solferino, the Cappello Ossuaria has the bones of over 7,000 men. The tower here pre-dates the battle by seven centuries, having been built by the Scaligeri, but it too now houses mementoes of the battle. There is a museum next to the tower with further items commemorating both the battle and the Risorgimento.

✚ 200 C1
Torre di San Martino e Museo
☎ 030 9910370 🕐 Mar–Sep daily 9–12.30, 2.30–7; Oct–Feb Tue–Sun 9–12.30, 2–4.30 💵 Moderate

Museo Della Croce Rossa
✉ Via Garibaldi 50, Castiglione delle Stiviere ☎ 0376 638505 🕐 Apr–Oct Tue–Sun 9–12, 3–6; Nov–Feb 9–12, 2–5 💵 Moderate

❺ Parco Giardino Sigurta

About 8km (5 miles) south of Peschiera is the Parco Giardino Sigurta, the work of Count Carlo Sigurta (1898–1983), Italy's answer to Britain's Capability Brown, who, using water from the Mincio River, converted 50ha (123 acres) of relatively barren country into a wonderful park with lakes, viewing terraces and Italianate gardens. The project took the count almost 50 years. His idea that world peace would follow mankind's acceptance of the beauties of nature and brotherhood may have been naïve, but there is no doubting the beauty and peace of Sigurta.

The modern sundial in the Parco Giardino Sigurta, near Peschiera

✚ Off 201 D1 ☎ 045 6371033
🕐 Early Mar–Nov daily 9–6. Visitors must leave by 7pm 💵 Expensive

❻ Peschiera del Garda

Peschiera, where the Mincio River drains Lake Garda, has always been strategically important. The Romans occupied it, and in medieval times there was a castle and a walled harbour. When the Austrians held the area they demolished the castle, but reinforced the walls, making Peschiera one corner of their defensive quadrilateral, the other corners being at Legnago, Mantova and

Verona. The Austrian defences remain and are still uncompromising, though overgrown. To see them properly, take a boat ride.

In the main square look for the town hall clock, with the beaks of two bronze eagles striking the hour.

✚ 201 D1

7 Gardaland

Gardaland, just north of Peschiera, is Italy's biggest and most popular theme park. New features are added each year to maintain the park's cutting edge, so any attempt to list them is bound to be out of date. But safe to say that if you have children and they like roller-coasters, water rides, fantasy characters, dolphins, safaris, play areas and much, much more, then they will love Gardaland. The park caters for children from 'just walking' upwards. Free pushchairs are available and there are plenty of refreshments.

✚ 201 D2 ☎ 045 6449777
🕐 Easter–Jun and last two weeks of Sep daily 10–6; Jul to mid-Sep 9–midnight; Oct Sat–Sun 9.30–6
💷 Expensive. Entrance is free for the carers of disabled visitors and children under 1m (3ft) tall. There is a reduced entry fee for under 10s and over 60s

8 Lazise

One of several pleasant villages on the Gardesana Orientale is Lazise, which has an arched and fortified town wall on three sides, with the lake on the fourth, and ruins of an old Scaligeri castle. Known as the 'key to the lake', this was an important Venetian fort with warships and a chain strung across the harbour entrance to prevent surprise attacks. The Palazzo dei Capitano (Customs House), which still stands, collected taxes on goods imported and exported from the harbour. The 12th-century church at the port, San Nicolò, has 14th-century frescoes.

✚ 201 D2

9 Bardolino

Bardolino is famous for the red wine that is produced locally. There is a museum of wine in the town and you can follow a route through the wine growing area (▶ 182–186). But Bardolino does not turn its back on the olives that name Garda's eastern shore and the Museo dell'Olio d'Oliva shows the processes that create extra virgin, virgin and the coarser grades.

The simple interior of the Church of San Severo, at Bardolino

As well as these two museums the town also has a couple of fine churches. San Zeno is an 8th-century Carolingian building (one of the oldest in Italy) with a crossing tower, while San Severo is Romanesque, dating from the 12th century. Inside there are stoutly columned arcades and 12th-century frescoes, and behind the high altar excavations have revealed an earlier Lombard church. San Severo also has a terrific campanile.

➕ 201 D3

Museo del Vino

✉ Via Costabella 9 ☎ 045 7210022
🕐 Mar–Oct daily 9–1, 2–6 🎟 Free

Museo dell'Olio d'Oliva

✉ Via Peschiera 54
☎ 045 6229047 🕐 Mar to mid-Jan daily 9–12.30, 2.30–7 (closed Sun pm)
🎟 Free

🔟 Punta di San Vigilio

At Garda a hook of land resembling a falcon's beak forms a sheltered bay called Punta di San Vigilio. At the tip of the hook are the private, 16th-century Villa Guarienti – a stunning building by Michele Sanmicheli

(1484–1559), an exclusive and expensive hotel (Locanda San Vigilio) overlooking a tiny harbour, and a little church (dedicated to San Vigilio). San Vigilio was a 13th-century hermit, but a local legend suggests an alternative for the name, claiming Vigilio was a satyr who loved a nymph, but turned her into the rock seen just offshore when she refused him. On the other side of the headland from the port is the tiny Baia delle Sirene (Serene Bay).

➕ 201 D3

🔢 Torri del Benaco

Another Scaligeri castle, still attached to a section of the old town walls, guards the headland that overlooks the eastern terminus of Lake Garda's only car ferry. The name derives from an earlier, Roman fortress. The imposing castle is now a museum documenting industries from local olive oil and lemon production to lake fishing and quarrying – Torri was once well-known for its red-yellow marble, used for many buildings in Verona, for example.

There is also a collection of prehistoric rock engravings from the area. The old lemon-trading house, Lemonaia, built in 1760, can also be

The Locanda San Vigilio hotel at Punta di San Vigilio

Very well-preserved frescoes inside the Church of Santa Trinità

visited: the house is one of few that now survive from the time when lemons were as important as olives to the Lake Garda economy.

You may also want to search out the Church of Santa Trinità, which has 14th-century frescoes in the style of Giotto.

➕ 201 D4
Museo del Castello Scaligero di Torre del Benaco and Lemonaia
☎ 045 6296111 🕐 Jun–Sep daily 9.30–1, 4.30–7.30; Apr–May and Oct 9.30–12.30, 2.30–6 💶 Moderate

🔢 Torbole

Torbole is one of the major centres on the lake for windsurfers and sailors, occasionally the blue of the lake water being almost completely obscured by multicoloured sails. It is also the first town in the Trentino region if you have followed the Gardesana Orientale northwards. It was from Torbole that fleets of

The harbourside at Torbole, originally an old fishing village

warships were launched in 1439 in the war between the Venetians and the Visconti. They had been dragged overland by teams of oxen (► 10).

If you are not a windsurfer you may well find Torbole's obsession with the sport overpowering, but there are other options nearby.

At Nago, 1.5km (1 mile) away, you can wander through the ruins of the Penede Castle at any time or admire the Marmitte dei Gigante, the Giant's Pots, a dozen smooth hollows scoured by the whirling of glacial meltwater on the Torbole–Nago road, about 1km (0.6 mile) from Torbole.

🞦 202 D2

🅱 Arco

In the 1870s the Archduke Albert of Habsburg Austria built a villa in Arco and spent a considerable amount of time there (eventually dying in the villa in 1895). The royal seal of approval brought other members of society and Arco became a fashionable resort. You can still admire the arboretum Albert planted around his villa and the casino where society whiled away its time and money.

A winding pathway (the walk takes about 20 minutes) leads up to the Castello di Arco, dating back to the 12th century and held by the Counts of Arco (though they, at various times, held it on behalf of the Veronese, Milanese and Venetians). It is mostly ruinous but some early frescoes are still visible: in one a chess game is in progress.

The castle stands above a sheer rock face, one of the foremost rock-climbing cliffs in Europe, on which competitions are sometimes held.

🞦 202 D3

Castello di Arco
🕓 Apr–Sep daily 10–6; Oct and Mar 10–4; Nov–Feb 10–3 💶 Moderate

Arboreto
☎ 0464 583608
🕓 Open daily 24 hours 💶 Free

Arco Castle, with perfect examples of the Scaligeri family's signature fishtail battlements

Where to... Stay

Prices
Expect to pay per double room, per night
€ under €70 €€ €70–€130 €€€ over €130

BARDOLINO

Hotel Benacus €€
All the bedrooms of this small hotel a short distance from the lake front have balconies, and there is a car park. No restaurant.
➕ 201 D3 ✉ Via Madonnina 11
☎ 045 6210282; www.hotelbenacus.it
🕑 Closed Dec–Mar

GARDA

Locanda San Vigilio €€€
In an exquisite position on Punta San Vigilio. Superbly furnished bedrooms, a private harbour, a sun terrace and much more.
➕ 201 D3 ✉ Punta San Vigilio
☎ 045 7256688;
www.punta-sanvigilio.it
🕑 Closed 15 Nov–15 Mar

LAZISE

Hotel da Roberto €€
A pleasant hotel occupying a Tyrolean-style building a short distance from the town centre.
➕ 201 D2 ✉ Via Verona Lago 24
☎ 045 7580065;
www.hoteldaroberto.com

MALCÉSINE

Hotel Aurora €
One of the most romantically sited hotels on the eastern shore, at the heart of Malcésine. Facilities are limited – though there is parking – but the rooms are comfortable and the staff friendly. No restaurant.
➕ 202 D1 ✉ Piazza Matteotti 10
☎ 045 7400114;
www.aurora-malcesine.com
🕑 Closed Nov–Mar

Hotel Castello €€
Below the castle and overlooking the best beach in town, this medium-size hotel has a relaxed and friendly atmosphere.
➕ 202 D1 ✉ Via Paina 3 ☎ 045 7400233; www.h-c.it 🕑 Closed mid-Nov to Mar

PEDEMONTE

Villa del Quar €€€
Away from the lake in the Valpolicella, this 16th-century villa is set in a vast park with private gardens and its own vineyard. Every conceivable desire is catered for.
➕ 201 F2 ✉ Via Quar 12 ☎ 045 6800681; www.hotelvilladelquar.it
🕑 Closed Nov–Mar. Restaurant closed Mon and Tue lunch

PESCHIERA DEL GARDA

Hotel Ristorante Bel Sito €€
Ideally positioned for excursions to local attractions and Verona. Swimming pool, garden and tennis court, and bikes can be hired.
➕ 201 D1 ✉ Via Venezia 62 ☎ 045 6400921; www.belsitohotel.com
🕑 Closed Nov

RIVA DEL GARDA

Grand Hotel Riva €€€
One of the lake's great hotels, the Grand successfully combines the old and the new. Chandeliers have been left, but the general décor updated. Large rooms, some with a stunning lake view. Sunloungers on the patio and a breakfast room overlooking the lake.
➕ 202 D3 ✉ Piazza Garibaldi 10
☎ 0464 521800; www.gardaresort.it

Where to...
Eat and Drink

Prices

Expect to pay for a three-course meal for one, excluding drinks and service

€ under €30   €€ €30–€60   €€€ over €60

Café Italia €

This is more a wine bar than a café, with a good selection of local wines to complement fresh dishes.

➕ 201 D3 ⌖ Piazza Principe Amedeo 2–4 ☎ 045 7211585 Ⓒ Closed Tue Mar–Oct and Mon–Fri Nov–Feb

Bussola Domani €

The owner makes the pasta and then you can choose between fish and meat for a main course. There is a garden at the back for outside dining.

➕ 201 D3 ⌖ Via Spagna 29 ☎ 045 7256475 Ⓒ Closed Nov–Mar

Trattoria Al Pescatore €

Tucked into a backstreet with some tables outside. Fish is a speciality and the menu is frequently changed. Good pizzas too.

➕ 201 D3 ⌖ Via Manzoni 23 ☎ 045 7256653 Ⓒ Closed mid-Nov to mid-Feb, Tue Oct and Mar–May

Alla Grotta €€

On the old harbour across from the Venetian Customs House and old church. Inside a large open fire is used, in part, to cook the food. Traditional Italian menu.

➕ 201 D2 ⌖ Via F Fontana 8 ☎ 045 7580035 Ⓒ Closed Tue

Corte Olivo €€

Built into a part of the old town walls. Tables in the garden in summer. Traditional menu and pizzas.

➕ 201 D2 ⌖ Corso Cangrande 22 ☎ 045 7581347 Ⓒ Closed Tue

Vecchia Malcésine €€

The menu is extensive and includes lake fish – try the poached pike – seafood and meat dishes, as well as traditional dishes with a twist. Huge wine list. Booking is advised.

➕ 202 D1 ⌖ Via Pisort 6 ☎ 045 7400469 Ⓒ Closed Wed, Feb and lunch Nov–Jan and Mar

La Torretta €€

Eat in a fine old building with wooden ceiling beams at the heart of old Peschiera – or sit outside under the sun umbrellas.

➕ 201 D1 ⌖ Via G Galilei 12 ☎ 045 7550108 Ⓒ Closed Wed

Binario €

A trendy restaurant with a varied and interesting menu. Good pizzas.

➕ 202 D3 ⌖ Largo Medaglie l'Oro ☎ 0464 520600 Ⓒ Closed Tue

Mediterraneo €€

Pleasant restaurant serving traditional Italian meals and pizzas cooked in a wood-burning stove.

➕ 202 D3 ⌖ Piazza Garibaldi 6 ☎ 0464 550175 Ⓒ Closed Tue

Where to... Shop

As with the towns of the western lake, the eastern shore towns are relatively small and have limited shopping potential.

BARDOLINO

August in Piazza Matteotti has a big choice of women's bags, shoes and clothes. For something different try the studio of **Maura Bontempi** in Piazza Statuto.

GARDA

For leather goods go to **Mola** (Corso Vittorio Emanuele 40). There is excellent jewellery at **Modini** (Corso Vittorio Emanuele 26) and at **Bella and Buona** (No 38) there is a tempting range of gifts.

For art, **Garda Ceramiche** (Via A Manzoni 20) has excellent ceramics while the **Studio per l'Arte** (Calle dei Sottoportici 6) is the studio of Adriano Foschi, an eclectic painter who also sells art material.

LAZISE

For ceramics, try **Il Gatto Nero** (Corso Ospedale 33). **Antico Mulino alla Torre** (Via Raffaello 35) displays Italian crafts, with jewellery, soaps and basketware, while **Clacson** (Corso Ospedale 28) has lovely children's clothes.

MALCÉSINE

Pelletteria Sophie (Via Parrocchia 5) has a good selection of handbags and other leatherware. For jewellery try **Voglia d'Oro** (Via Capitanito 1). There are few art outlets in town. The best is **Onice** (Corso Garibaldi 53) which specialises in ceramics.

Finally, head for **Casanova**

(Vicolo di Mezzo 5) for a good range of lace, candles, oils and gifts.

PESCHIERA DEL GARDA

It is worth checking **Piu Gioielli** (Via Rocca 21) for jewellery and silverware; **Antichità** (Via Cavallotti) across from the tourist office, for antiques, and **Candela d'Arte Giesse** (Piazza Bettelloni 14), next to the tourist office, for hand-made candles.

RIVA DEL GARDA

For something different try **Fronte Lago** (Viale San Francesco 9), which has weird but wonderful bags and scarves.

For jewellery head for **Easy Gold** (Via Santa Maria 3), **Orafo** (Via Monatanara 16), which specialises in gold, or **Re Artu Bijoux** (Via Lipella), which has ultra-modern jewellery.

Finally look out for **Le Petit Montmarte** (Via Fiume 71), the

studio of J N Versini, a whimsical artist, and **Loreini** (Via Diaz), which has colourful crystal and glass.

TORBOLE

Coast to Coast (Via Lungolago Verona), is good for young fashion items, while **Gioielleria Santoni** (also in Via Lungolago Verona), has fine jewellery.

MARKETS

Bardolino – Thursday; **Garda** – Friday; **Lazise** – Wednesday; **Malcésine** – Saturday; **Peschiera del Garda** – Monday; **Riva del Garda** – second and fourth Wednesdays of the month (June to September); second Wednesday only from October to May; **Torbole** – Tuesday; **Torri del Benaco** – Monday. Antiques markets at **Bardolino** on every third Sunday, and at **Torri del Benaco** on Wednesdays in summer.

Where to...
Be Entertained

SPORT AND LEISURE

Watersports

There is a large number of wind-surfing and sailing schools at the northern end of the lake. For wind-surfing, the best schools are **Surf Segnana** (at the Hotel du Lac, tel: 0464 552453) in Riva del Garda, and **Circolo Surf** (tel: 0464 505385), **Conca d'Oro Windsurf** (tel: 0464 548192), **Surfcenter Lido Blu** (at Hotel Lido Blu, tel: 0464 506349) and **Surf Segnana** (at Hotel Paradiso, tel: 0464 505963) in Torbole.

For sailing contact **Fraglia Vela Riva** (tel: 0464 552460), **Sailing Club Riva** (0464 552453), **Lega Navale Italiana** (tel: 0464 555201)

or **Gardaseecharter** (tel: 335 5274455) in Riva del Garda, or **Circolo Vela Torbole** (tel: 0464 506240) and **Surf Segnana** (tel: 0464 505963) in Torbole.

There is a diving school at Riva del Garda – **Gruppo Sommozzatori**, at Porto S Nicolò (tel: 0464 555120).

Canoe tuition/hire is available from **Canoa Club Canottieri Riva** (tel: 0464 555294).

Adventure Sports

Several organisations for rock climbing, canyoning and paragliding are available in Riva del Garda, Torbole and Arco, at the northern end of the lake. A list is available from the local tourist offices.

For canyoning, contact **Canyon Adventures** (tel: 0464 505406) in Torbole.

Golf

The 18-hole **Club Paradiso del Garda** at Peschiera del Garda (tel: 0365 954447) is the only course on the eastern shore.

FESTIVALS

At Lazise in June there is a **festival of medieval games**.

At Peschiera and Bardolino there are **wine festivals** in June.

Peschiera also has a **palio** in August in which two- and four-oared boats race along the town's canals.

The **Young Musicians' Festival** is held annually at the end of July in Riva del Garda.

Malcésine has a series of **music evenings** (8.30–10pm) during the summer – in Piazza Cavour on Mondays, in Piazza del Porto on Tuesdays, Thursdays and Sundays, and in Piazza Matteotti on Fridays.

NIGHTLIFE

Of the eastern towns on Lake Garda, Riva is the place to go for the most frenetic nightlife. There are discos at the **Novecento** (Via Gazzoletti) and **No Name** (Piazza Catena). If it's a pub or bar with music you want to visit for an evening out then try **Pub all'Oca** (Via Santa Maria 9), **Pub C9** (Viale dei Tigli 37), **Pub Lochness** (Viale Dante), and the **Barracuda** (Via dei Fabbri 11). The **New History Jungle Pub** (8–10 Via Montanara) claims to serve 100 cocktails.

At Torbole there are discos/pubs with live music at **Pub MC Fly Snack** (Via Matteoti 25), and the **Cutty Sark Pub** (Via Pontalti 2).

Away from the northern lake the opportunities are more limited, but the **Taverna Norma** (Viale F Lavanda 13, Torri del Benaco), is a wine bar with live music.

Verona

Getting Your Bearings

The city of Romeo and Juliet; the city where operas are performed in the open air in a lavishly decorated Roman amphitheatre; the city where, from their tombs, former lords peer out at visitors.

In a country of extraordinary cities – Rome, Florence, Venice – cities such as Verona seem commonplace. Yet the medieval heart of Verona is as well preserved and as interesting as those of its more illustrious cousins, and if the art on show here is not at the forefront of the Renaissance masterworks, the Roman remains and Shakespearean associations are enough to compensate.

Romeo and Juliet might not have lived in Verona. Indeed, they might not have lived at all, but it was probably a local legend that formed the basis of Shakespeare's tragedy. Some of the sites that are now claimed to be the 'authentic' sites from the play are not of course, but though they may to have been invented with an eye to the tourist trade, many have the feel of authenticity: if Juliet did not call Romeo from the balcony in that house in Via Cappello, then she should have done.

There is no such credibility problem with the Roman amphitheatre, which is most definitely 1,900 years old.

The lords who gaze down at you in Piazza dei Signori have curious names. The Scaligeri (della Scala) family that ruled medieval Verona descended from Mastino della Scala. As *mastino* is Italian for mastiff, later lords took the prefix *can* – dog – as a tribute. There was a Cangrande – big dog – and a Cansignorio – lord dog. But there were black sheep in the family too and one member was Canrabbiaso – mad dog.

The triple-arched Ponte Scaligero over the River Adige in Verona. It was built as an escape route in the event of the Castelvecchio falling to enemy hands

★ Don't Miss

1. **Piazza dei Signori** ➤ 92
2. **Piazza Erbe** ➤ 94
3. **Piazza Bra** ➤ 96
4. **San Zeno Maggiore** ➤ 98

Holy water stoup in Sant' Anastasia

At Your Leisure

5. Castelvecchio and Ponte Scaligero ➤ 100
6. Tomba di Giulietta ➤ 100
7. San Fermo Maggiore ➤ 100
8. Casa di Giulietta ➤ 101
9. Santa Maria Antica ➤ 101
10. Sant' Anastasia ➤ 103
11. Duomo ➤ 103
12. Museo Archeologico and Teatro Romano ➤ 104
13. Giardino Giusti ➤ 104
14. San Giorgio in Braida ➤ 104

Explore Verona's main sights – tucked into a loop south of the Adige River – comfortably in a day.

In a Day
Morning
10am

Having had breakfast – either at your hotel or perhaps in a café close to the river – head for the **11 Duomo** (below, ➤ 103). This is your first stop; after admiring the structure of the building, go inside to see the artwork, looking especially for the Titian masterpiece .

From the cathedral take Via Duomo, which heads southeast, following it past the **Museo d'Arte** (➤ 100), to your right, to reach the huge **10 Church of Sant' Anastasia** (➤ 103) with its soaring interior. Step inside to admire the art, particularly the Pisanello.

11am

Continue along Via Duomo, then turn right into Via delle Arche Scaligeri, soon passing the Casa di Romeo. This austere 14th-century house is known to have belonged to the Montecchi family, which Shakespeare anglicised to Montague, and has become, inevitably, Romeo's House. Continue to the **9 Santa Maria Antica** (➤ 101) and then go through the arch to reach **8 Piazza dei Signori** (➤ 92–93).

11.45am

Having paid your respects to Dante (➤ 92–93) and admired the surrounding buildings, climb the Torre dei Lamberti for a view down into Piazza Erbe.

12.30pm

Mind your head as you go under the whale-bone (➤ 93) to reach **2 Piazza Erbe** (➤ 94–95). As well as many stalls selling, among other things, Carnival masks (left), there is plenty of choice here for an early lunch. Alternatively, wait till you reach Piazza Bra. After a quick stroll around the square, take Via Cappello, which exits from

the southeastern corner (turn left as you enter from Piazza dei Signori).
Soon you will reach, to the left, **8 Casa di Giulietta** (➤ 101),
with its evocative balcony.

1.30pm

From Casa di Giulietta continue along Via Cappello, then turn first right
along Via Stella, following it to **3 Piazza Bra** (➤ 96–97). If you haven't
already eaten, choose one of the pavement cafés/restaurants that line the
Listone for lunch – perhaps the Olivo restaurant/pizzeria at No 18a or
the Liston, another restaurant/pizzeria at No 19 – admiring the outside
of the Arena (below) and, probably, the street-theatre artists.

Afternoon

2.45pm

Visit the **Arena** (➤ 96–97). A visit takes about an hour. Afterwards, walk
back along the Listone, then turn right along Via Roma to reach the
5 Castelvecchio and Ponte Scaligero (➤ 100). A good exploration of
the site will take about two hours.

4.45pm

Reverse your route to the Listone and have a coffee at Café Opera
(No 10c). The crowds thin at this time of day so you will be able to relax
and consider whether to visit the stalls in Piazza Erbe before they close,
or enjoy the shopping in Via Mazzini before choosing a
restaurant for the evening.

❶ Piazza dei Signori

At the heart of old Verona, a marvellous jumble of narrow streets and alleys, two squares represent the diverse faces of Renaissance Italy. Piazza Erbe is for the ordinary folk, but Piazza dei Signori (Square of the Gentlemen) is where power was exercised. In keeping with that role the piazza is much more formal, perfectly rectangular and with a harmony that is truly stately. At the centre is a statue of Dante sculpted by Ugo Zannoni in the 1860s, a reminder of the time the poet spent in exile in Verona as a guest of Bartolomeo I della Scala. Dante was not renowned as a fun-loving optimist and Zannoni has captured him, fittingly, in sombre mood.

Loggia del Consiglio

Over the poet's left shoulder is the Loggia del Consiglio, the finest of the square's buildings and former seat of Verona's council. It is occasionally called the Loggia del Fra'Giacondo because legend has it that it was designed by a Veronese monk. The building dates from the late 15th century though it was not finally completed until 300 years later. The design, with its arcading and mullioned windows, has Tuscan echoes, but is now considered the first flowering of Veronese Renaissance.

On the roof of the Loggia del Consiglio there are statues of the city's great sons from the Roman era

Palazzo della Prefettura

On one side of the loggia an arch links it to the 15th-century Casa della Pieta. On the other, forming a corner of the square, is the Palazzo della Prefettura, built in the 14th century and restored to its original design in the 1920s. Once the palazzo

Below: the
interior court-
yard of the
Palazzo del
Commune

Below right:
Dante's statue
by Ugo
Zannoni,
sculpted in
the 1860s

of Verona's rulers, it is finished with the fishtail battlements of the Scaligeri, added not as decoration but to ensure that everyone knew who was in charge. During his exile Dante stayed here. Giotto is also reputed to have been a guest.

Dante gazes across towards the Cortile dei Tribunale, reached by a narrow passageway. To the left of this is the Palazzo del Capitano, built in the 14th century and with another doorway by Sanmicheli. There is another interesting doorway in the courtyard where you will also be able to look down through glass covers at an excavated section of street from Roman Verona. The Prefettura and Capitano are linked by the narrow, arched Piazzaletto della Arche, which leads to the Scaligeri tombs and the **Church of Santa Maria Antica** (➤ 101).

Palazzo della Ragione

On the other side of Via Dante is the Palazzo della Ragione, after the loggia the most attractive building in the piazza. The striking red (brick) and white (stone) horizontal stripes are a feature of Veronese buildings, having been a popular architectural form in the early Renaissance period. The façade of the building facing the piazza is plain, but the inner courtyard, the Cortile del Mercato Vecchio (the Old Market), is a complete contrast. Rising from the cobbled market square is an ornate two-tiered stairway known as 'Stairway of Reason' because the courts and prison lay at the top of it. Above the stairway rises the **Torre dei Lamberti** (➤ 95).

TAKING A BREAK

In the square itself the only place to eat is the **Impero trattoria/pizzeria** at No 8. However, **Alla Costa**, just beyond the arch into Piazza Erbe, is a good pizzeria.

➕ 199 D2

PIAZZA DEI SIGNORI: INSIDE INFO

Top tip Scavi Scaligeri, the excavated Roman streets that lie beneath the Palazzo del Capitano, occasionally houses **photographic exhibitions**. This is a great way of seeing both the streets and some fine works.

Hidden gem Piazza dei Signori is linked to Piazza Erbe by the **Arco della Costa**, the 'arch of the rib'. The rib in question is a whalebone suspended beneath the arch. Legend has it that it will fall on the first honest man who walks beneath it.

2 Piazza Erbe

In contrast to the elegant formality of Piazza dei Signori, Piazza Erbe is chaotic, its shape irregular, its buildings an architectural mish-mash, its atmosphere frantic. This is the Square of Herbs, named after the plants that were once the only item sold here. Now the white umbrellas of the stall-holders protect all manner of things from the sun. The square is still a food market, but here too are clothing and tourist souvenirs, and enough objets d'art and bric-à-brac to keep a collector happy for many hours.

The square is built on what was the Roman forum and is roughly rectangular, though the side away from Piazza dei Signori is angled into and away from Via Pellicciai. On the corner of that street is the Casa dei Mercanti, built in the early 14th century as the merchant's hall and still, 700 years later, the city's chamber of commerce, though the building has undergone several modifications and restorations so that the mullioned windows and crenellations are all that can claim to be original.

The Monuments

Close to the Casa dei Mercanti is the first of four monuments that lie on a straight line through the square, the central pair poking out above the umbrella cover. This first is the 15th-century Colonna del Mercato, a Gothic stone lantern. The next is the 16th-century loggia known as the Berlina or Capitello. Here the inauguration of city officials took place and, on less solemn occasions, locals guilty of misde-meanours, who had therefore escaped prison or the gallows, were pelted by rotten fruit and vegetables. The third monu-ment is the curious Fontana di Madonna Verona, built by Cansignorio della Scala in 1368. It is topped by a Roman statue. Found headless and restored in somewhat bizarre fashion, the statue is now revered by the Veronese. The last monument is a tall column topped by the Lion of St Mark, the symbol of the Venetian Republic. When the Veronese revolted against French rule during the Pasque Veronesi of 1797 the lion was torn down and smashed, but has been restored.

Other Fine Buildings

Behind the Venetian lion is Palazzo Maffei, a 17th-century

Top: looking down into Piazza Erbe from the top of Torre dei Lamberti

Above: summer fruits for sale in the piazza

Left: the Lion of St Mark

baroque building with its upper balustrade surmounted by six statues of Roman gods. Beside it is the Torre del Gardello, another 14th-century building by Cansignorio. Though it is tall and slender there was room at the top for a few della Scala fishtails. Diagonally across from Palazzo Maffei is Casa Mazzanti. Built in the 14th century as a palace for the ruling Scaligeri, it was significantly altered in the 16th century when the frescoes were added. Beside it the Domus Nova was also originally built in the 14th century, but then radically reconstructed, this time in the 17th century. It was home to the medieval city's chief magistrate.

Torre dei Lamberti

At the other end of the Piazza Erbe is Torre dei Lamberti, which gives a panoramic view of the square. Begun in 1172 as a symbol of the power of the city, but not completed for 300 years, the tower is 84m (275ft) high and is the best viewpoint in Verona. There is a lift to the top, accessed from the courtyard of the Palazzo della Ragione (➤ 93).

TAKING A BREAK

You are spoilt for choice in the square and adjacent streets. The **Mezzaparte** at No 8a serves the best hot chocolate, while the **Orchidea** at No 22 is a good *gelateria*/café.

🔢 199 D2
Torre dei Lamberti
☎ 045 9273027 ⏰ Mon 1.30–8, Tue–Sun 9.30–8 (or dusk) 💰 Moderate

---

PIAZZA ERBE: INSIDE INFO

Top tip Piazza Erbe is oriented northwest/southeast, so the **best time to climb Torre dei Lamberti** for views and photography is late morning, when the sun shines along the square's length.

Hidden gem In the small square beside the Casa dei Mercanti there is a **monument to the Veronesi** killed by an Austrian bomb dropped during the 1914–18 war, one of the first air attacks on civilians.

③ Piazza Bra

The wide, spacious Piazza Bra (one of the largest squares in Italy), standing at the southern edge of the old town, takes its name from the Latin *pratum* (meadow), because the Arena stood outside the city walls in Roman times. At its centre is a small area of parkland around a fountain.

Across the park from the Arena is the huge Palazzo della Gran Guardia, a fine early 17th-century building with Doric columns whose design was clearly influenced by the work of Sanmicheli. He also designed the Palazzo Guastaverza, which forms part of the Listone (No 16). The Gran Guardia was constructed, in part, from stone from the Arena: behind it rises a tower (Torre Pentagona), a reminder of the time between Scaligeri and Venetian rule when Milan's Visconti were the lords of Verona. From the Gran Guardia, an arch, the Portoni delle Bra, a remaining section of the old Visconti city walls, crosses the road to the Museo Lapidarium Maffeiano (Museum of Maffei's Lapidary).

The Arena

The Arena, Verona's Roman amphitheatre, standing on the eastern side of Piazza Bra, is the most famous of the city's buildings and, though not complete, one of the best of its kind still surviving. The amphitheatre is elliptical and, at 152m (165 yards) long, 123m (134 yards) wide and 30m (33 yards) high it was exceeded in size only by Rome's Colosseum. It was built in the first century in a combination of brick and pink stone quarried in the Valpolicella. Originally it had two external walls, the inner comprising 74 double arcades, all of which still stand. Outside this stood a wall of triple arcades but a series of earthquakes, the most destructive of which was in 1183, and the more mundane use of the stone as a convenient quarry by local builders, means that only a single section of four triple arcades remains. Known as the *ala* (wing), this section is a well-loved local landmark.

Within the walls the *cavea* comprises 44 tiers (some restored to their original form) which can seat about 25,000 spectators around an arena floor measuring 74m (81 yards) by 44m (48 yards). Originally the spectators would have watched typical Roman games, gladiators occasionally dying on

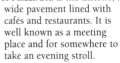

the sand-strewn floor. Later, tournaments, duels and other medieval festivals would have taken place here, the Arena only being taken over for theatrical events late in its life. One of the actresses who performed here, taking the role of Juliet, was Eleanor Duse, the mistress and muse of Gabriele d'Annunzio, whose Il Vittoriale stands beside Lake Garda at Gardone (➤ 50–52).

Since 1913 the Arena has been used for an annual opera season for which it has become world famous, not only for the quality of the performances but for the fantastic designs and scale of the sets.

Bottom left: advertising for performances at the Roman Arena (below), once used for games and gladiatorial contests

The Listone

Forming the northwestern side of Piazza Bra is the Listone, a wide pavement lined with cafés and restaurants. It is well known as a meeting place and for somewhere to take an evening stroll.

TAKING A BREAK

Choose any of the cafés/restaurants on the Listone. The **Café Opera** at No 10c is excellent for coffee, while the **Olivo restaurant/pizzeria** at No 18a is good for lunch.

➕ 199 D2
Arena
☎ 045 8003204 ⏰ Mon 1.30–7.30, Tue–Sun 8.30–7.30. During the opera season the Arena closes at 2pm
💶 Moderate

Museo Lapidarium Maffeiano
☎ 045 590087 ⏰ Tue–Sun 8.30–1.30 💶 Moderate

PIAZZA BRA: INSIDE INFO

Top tip As well as being one of the best places in Verona for people-watching, the Listone is the venue of choice for some of the city's best **street-theatre performers**. For good entertainment, have a few euros ready, buy a coffee and wait.

Hidden gems Most visitors do not realise they can climb on to the **Portoni della Bra**. Although it is not always open, it gives a great view of the Listone.
• In the **Museo Lapidarium Maffeiano**, find your way to the Roman funeral reliefs, which are among the best and certainly the most moving of the engraved stones.

❹ San Zeno Maggiore

Almost everything worth seeing in Verona lies within the tight loop of the Adige River, which virtually encircles the old town. But there are exceptions and chief among these is the Basilica of San Zeno, 800m (872 yards) east of the Arena.

San Zeno was a 4th-century, African-born saint, who built the first church on this site. What you now see is arguably the finest Romanesque building in Italy, dating from the 12th century. To the left of the church, the red tower is all that remains of a Benedictine monastery. To the right is a taller, more slender campanile.

Before entering the church, look up to see the **Wheel of Fortune** rose windows that pierce the façade, a 12th-century masterpiece by 'Maestro Brioloto'. Inside, the church is divided into three by stark arcading. The central nave is tall and elegantly roofed and leads to a two-tier sanctuary. Below is the **colonnaded crypt** where the remains of San Zeno rest among the sarcophagi of other early medieval saints. Above the crypt is the church's most precious possession, a triptych altarpiece of the Madonna and Saints by Andrea Mantegna. The predella is actually a copy, the original having been snaffled by Napoleon for the Louvre in Paris. Nearby is a polychrome statue of a laughing San Zeno.

Easy to overlook are the 48 **bronze panels** on the entrance door. Once thought to represent the worst aspect of primitive medieval art, these 11th-century works are now seen as masterpieces. The subjects are biblical scenes and the miracles of San Zeno, depicted with a naivety that would have helped convey their message to the congregation.

Another thing to look out for is the porphyry bowl in the

Detail of the church's door panels (top) and the cloisters and campanile (above)

Did You Know?

The city's *carraccio* (war wagon) once stood in the left nave of the Basilica of San Zeno Maggiore. Drawn by oxen, the wagon preceded the city's troops into battle. On it were relics of the city's patron saint – San Zeno – priests praying for victory and a rebel-rousing band of drums and trumpets to enthuse the soldiers. The capture of an opponent's *carraccio* was a humiliating blow for the losers. Today a *carraccio* still carries the *palio*, the prize banner, into Siena's campo before the famous horse race.

Statues of Christ and the Apostles, dating from the 13th century

left nave. One legend has it that the bowl was presented by San Zeno to the Roman Emperor, while another suggests it was put here by the Devil (though why he should have done so is not clear).

TAKING A BREAK

There is a café across from the old tower, on the corner of Vicolo Abazia, but for something more substantial try the **Trattoria Al Calmiere** farther along in Piazza San Zeno.

🔢 199 D2
🕐 Mon–Sat 8.30–6, Sun 1–6

SAN ZENO MAGGIORE: INSIDE INFO

Top tip San Zeno is on the itinerary of every **coach tour** to Verona, but the first coaches do not arrive until mid-morning. As the church opens at 8.30am, arrive early to enjoy a peaceful visit.

At Your Leisure

The stage is set: two armoured knights contribute to a theatrical production in front of the Castelvecchio battlements

5 Castelvecchio and Ponte Scaligero

In the mid-14th century Cangrande II built the 'old castle' as both a house and a fortress, beside the Adige so that the river could enhance the defences. At first a symbol of Scaligeri power and ownership, the castle was later used by the Venetians as a college and by the French and Austrians as a barracks.

The castle, with its massive, forbidding towers and fishtail battlements, is a superb example of early medieval war architecture, but is now used for a gentler purpose, as Verona's **Museo d'Arte**. The collection, spanning the 14th to 18th centuries, is impressive and includes works by Paolo Veronese, Pisanello, Mantegna and Tintoretto. Sculptures include an agonizing Crucifixion by an unknown maestro and a relief-carved sarcophagus. There is also a stunning collection of arms and armour, and the original equestrian statue of Cangrande I from the Scaligeri tombs. Though highly stylised, the statue of cloth-decked

horse and armoured lord – how heavy must that helmet have been to wear? – is very dramatic.

From the castle the **Ponte Scaligero** crosses the Adige, an elegant triple-arched bridge with fishtail battlements. Apparently built as an escape route just in case the castle fell, the bridge was almost completely destroyed in World War II, but was later restored.

Castelvecchio
🏰 199 D2 ☎ 045 8062611
🕐 Mon 1.30–6.45, Tue–Sun 8.30–6.45
💶 Moderate

6 Tomba di Giulietta

Close to the river in Via del Pontieri, about 350m (382 yards) south of the Arena, is the Tomba di Giulietta, a 14th-century red marble sarcophagus which, tradition has it, was the last resting place of Shakespeare's heroine. Legend also says that Romeo and Juliet were married in the Franciscan monastery that once stood here, but there is no more truth in this than in the legend linking Juliet with the sarcophagus in the baroque chapel. But as with Juliet's House, the site feels right, and that feeling is shared by the many who come here to drop love letters in the sarcophagus or coins in the courtyard fountain.

Attached to the site is the **Museo degli Affreschi**, a small museum of medieval frecoes.

Tomba di Giulietta/Museo degli Affreschi
🏰 199 D2 ✉ Via del Pontiere 35
☎ 045 8000361 🕐 Mon 1.30–6.45,
Tue–Sun 8.30–6.45 💶 Moderate

7 San Fermo Maggiore

North of Juliet's tomb, in a square at the town end of the Ponte Navi, stands the **Church of San Fermo**

Maggiore. Built on the site where San Fermo and San Rusticus were martyred in 361, the church is actually two, one built on top of the other. The lower, Romanesque, church was built by Benedictine monks in the 13th century, the upper, Gothic, church being added by Franciscans 250 years later. The façade shows the familiar horizontal striping, while the original campanile is now crowded with Gothic apses.

To the left side of the façade doorway a funeral monument remembers the 14th-century doctor who kept the Scaligeri lords healthy. The upper church has a terrific wooden roof and several artistic masterpieces. Among these is a frescoed Annunciation by Pisanello. The sculpted pulpit and its surrounding frescoes are also outstanding.

The lower church is a contrast, a simple, dignified, multi-arcaded building. Here too there are some good frescoes and a marvellous wooden Crucifixion.

🚹 199 D2

8 Casa di Giulietta

The claim of the Casa di Giulietta, in Via Cappello, to be the actual home of Shakespeare's Juliet rests on the

Many would-be Romeos and Juliets have posed for the camera on this balcony

fact that it was once an inn called Il Cappello and the bard based his story on the old tale of a feud between the local families of Cappello or Cappelletti (Capulets) and Montecchi (Montagues). But flimsy evidence is readily cast aside, because here, as at Juliet's tomb, the place feels right. The balcony might be too high for a youthful Romeo to have reached, but young love knows no bounds, as countless young ladies who have their photographs taken while dreaming of young admirers will testify.

The house is probably 13th century and so is about the right period, and the commercialism that can swamp such sites is adequately restrained. Perhaps the only unfortunate aspects are the crowds that can overwhelm a contemplative visit and the statue of Juliet – too modern and too mature to be a girl barely into her teens.

🚹 199 D2 ✉ Via Capello 23 🕐 Mon 1.30–6.45, Tue–Sun 8.30–6.45 ☎ 045 8034303 🎫 Moderate

9 Santa Maria Antica

The old church – 12th-century, but much restored – is a fine Romanesque building, but serves only as a backdrop to the main attraction, the elaborate tomb to Cangrande I and, beside it, the

Left: Verona's cityscape, dominated by the Duomo's campanile

fenced off collection of tombs to other members of the della Scala dynasty. Cangrande I, who died in 1329, is shown in effigy above his sarcophagus, beneath which crowned dogs hold shields showing the ladders (*scala*) symbolising the family name. The tomb, which is also the porch of the church, is topped by a replica of the equestrian statue in the Castelvecchio.

On all the other tombs the theme of Cangrande I's tomb is maintained, each showing both an effigy and an equestrian statue of the Scaligeri lord. Of the others, the most elaborate is that of Cansignorio, who died in 1375, with its delicate stone tracery and canopied sword bearers.

🕇 199 D2

🔟 Sant' Anastasia

Verona's largest church, a little way north of the Scaligeri tombs, was begun in 1290 but never completed, as a glance at the façade readily confirms. But if the outside is disappointing, the inside is most definitely not, the soaring Gothic arches and patterned floor being a joy. Near the entrance two holy water stoups are held aloft by gobbi, hunchbacked figures bent double by their loads. Despite their ugliness, the humanity of the figures has made them one of the best-loved works in any local church.

Roman columns at the Teatro Romano

Sant' Anastasia also has more formal works of art, including an important 14th-century fresco by Altichiero, a follower of Giotto, of the Cavalli family. The fresco is in the Cavalli Chapel. There is also a famous work by Pisanello, *St George and the Princess*, considered by many to be his masterpiece, though it seems strange that he placed the rear end of the horse so prominently in the ensemble

🕇 199 D2

🕕 Duomo

Set beside the river, Verona's cathedral is a mix of forms, Romanesque at its base, Gothic above and with a campanile begun in medieval times and completed in 1926. The portal is by Nicolò, who also created the portal of San Zeno.

Inside, the cathedral is vast, but exquisitely well balanced. A pope is buried here, Lucius III preferring Verona to Rome and so shifting the papal seat here from 1181 until his death in 1185 (sadly just two years before the cathedral's dedication).

The pope's death mask is on display, but there are less macabre works, including the only painting Titian completed in the city. His *Assumption* is the altarpiece of the Nichesola Chapel, the first in the left nave. In it the Madonna looks sorrowfully down at the grieving throng – made up entirely of men – who watch her departure.

🕇 199 D2 ☎ 045 592813 🕐 Mar–Oct Mon–Sat 10–5.30; Nov–Feb Tue–Sat 10–4; Sun and public hols 1.30–5

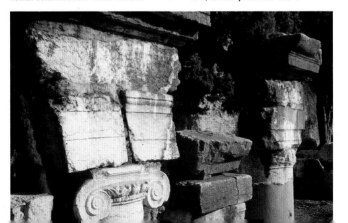

🄻 Museo Archeologico and Teatro Romano

A short distance from the Duomo is the Ponte Pietra, one of the city's two Roman bridges. Only two of the arches were original, however (the others having been rebuilt in medieval times) when the bridge was blown up during World War II. Pieces were later dredged from the riverbed and reconstructed.

as the gardens of the Palazzo Giusti, they are among the most beautiful and famous in Italy. The lower section is formal, with hedging, lawns, statues and fountains.

On the hillside is a more natural area from a redesign of the 19th century. The cypresses are such a feature of this section that Goethe is said to have taken branches from them during his visit as a permanent

Box hedging and cypress trees at the typically Italianate Giusti Gardens

Over the bridge and to the right is the Roman theatre, built in the early 1st century and still used for its original purpose during a summer season of plays. But the use has not been continuous: the theatre became overgrown and was not rediscovered until 250 years ago.

From the theatre you can take a lift to the old convent on the hilltop. Now converted into a small museum, it houses a collection of Etruscan, Roman and Greek antiquities.

➕ 199 D2 ✉ Via Redentore 2 ☎ 045 8000360 🕐 Mon 1.30–6.45, Tue–Sun 8.30–6.45 💷 Moderate

🄼 Giardino Giusti

Beyond the Roman theatre are the Giusti Gardens. Begun in about 1580

reminder. The gardens are favoured by wedding couples as they make a perfect backdrop for photos.

➕ 199 D2 ✉ Via Giardino Giusti 2 ☎ 045 8034029 🕐 Apr–Sep daily 9–8; Oct–Mar daily 9–7 💷 Expensive

🄽 San Giorgio in Braida

If, instead of turning right at the end of Ponte Pietra, you bear left beside the river you will reach the domed Church of San Giorgio in Braida. Built in the 15th century on the site of an earlier church, the prominent dome was added by Sanmicheli 200 years later. Inside there are a number of fine art works, including what many believe to be Paolo Veronese's masterpiece, *The Martyrdom of St George*, and a *Baptism of Christ* by Jacopo Tintoretto.

➕ 199 D2

Where to... Stay

Prices

Expect to pay per double room, per night

€ under €70   **€€** €70–€130   **€€€** over €130

Accademia €€€

Right at the heart of the historic centre, the Accademia is just a short walk from Juliet's House. It occupies a 17th-century palazzo and combines antique furnishings with modern facilities. Private rooms are elegant and well appointed and the restaurant is excellent.

➕ 199 D2 ◻ Via Scala 12 ☎ 045 596222; www.accademiavr.it

Aurora €€

The Aurora, a small, neat hotel in Piazza Erbe, could hardly be more centrally, or romantically, positioned. Good, straightforward and comfortable accommodation and friendly staff.

Bologna €€€

Occupies a lovely old building in a quiet area just a short walk from the Arena. Well-appointed rooms, friendly staff and secure parking.

➕ 199 D2 ◻ Piazzetta Sealette Rubiani 3 ☎ 045 8006830; www.hotelbologna.vr.it

De Capuleti €€

Close to Juliet's tomb and so about 10 minutes' walk from the Arena, this establishment is family run and very friendly. It has been modernised to a high standard. Secure parking.

➕ 199 D2 ◻ Piazza Erbe ☎ 045 594717; www.hotelaurora.bis

➕ 199 D2 ◻ Via del Pontiere 26 ☎ 045 8000154; www.hotelcapuleti.it

Due Torri Hotel Baglioni €€€

A 13th-century palazzo close to the Church of Sant'Anastasia is now Verona's most exclusive hotel. The public rooms with their arches and stylish bedrooms are the height of elegance, and every possible convenience is provided. The restaurant is, as would be expected, first class.

➕ 199 D2 ◻ Piazza Sant' Anastasia 4 ☎ 045 595044; www.baglionihotels.com

Giulietta e Romeo €€€

Just 50m (55 yards) away from the Arena and so at the very heart of the old city, yet the Giulietta e Romeo can be reached by car and has secure parking. You can borrow a bicycle if you wish. Small and friendly. No restaurant, but there is plenty of choice locally.

➕ 199 D2 ◻ Vicolo Tre Marchetti 3 ☎ 045 8003554; www.giuliettaeromeo.com

Grand Hotel €€€

The Grand is very well positioned on the road linking the city centre with the A4 *autostrada* and is just a few minutes' walk from Piazza Bra. There is a striking reception area and delightful private courtyard garden.

➕ 199 D2 ◻ Corso Porta Nuova 105 ☎ 045 595600; www.grandhotel.vr.it

San Marco €€€

Close to San Zeno Maggiore and so a 20-minute walk, or short bus ride, from the main centre, the hotel occupies an old house and a modern extension. Breakfast is served in the garden. There is also a pool.

➕ 199 D2 ◻ Via Longhena 42 ☎ 045 569011; www.sanmarco.vr.it

Verona €€

The hotel prides itself on attention to detail and it shows, with well-appointed rooms and public areas.

➕ 199 D2 ◻ Corso Porta Nuova 47/49 ☎ 045 595944; www.hotelverona.it

Where to...
Eat and Drink

Prices
Expect to pay for a three-course meal for one, excluding drinks and service
€ under €30   €€ €30–€60   €€€ over €60

Al Cristo €€
Close to Ponte Nuovo and so a little away from the city centre, this restored 16th-century palazzo is worth the walk for its delightful atmosphere. Good fish and meat dishes served on a terrific terrace.
➕ 199 D2 ⊠ Piazzetta Peschiera 6
☎ 045 594287;
www.ristorantealcristo.it
⊘ Closed Mon

Antica Bottega del Vino €€
Tucked away off Via Mazzini, the Antica Bottega del Vino is wonderfully atmospheric with its bottle-lined walls. Specialities include a chef's tortellini, polenta dishes and horse meat. The wine list runs to about 100 pages. The service is superb.
➕ 199 D2 ⊠ Via Scudo di Francia 3
☎ 045 8004535 ⊘ Closed Tue except during opera season

Aquila Nera Café €
A tempting buffet is served here either for lunch or pre-opera during the season. It is just off Piazza Erbe.
➕ 199 D2 ⊠ Galleria Pellicciaiz
☎ 045 8010172

Arche €€€
One of the best restaurants in Verona, with a prime position close to the Scaligeri tombs. Fresh fish arrives daily for the evening menu which comprises both unusual and traditional dishes. Booking advised.
➕ 199 D2 ⊠ Via Arche Scaligeri 6
☎ 045 8007415 ⊘ Closed Sun and Mon lunch

La Costa in Bra €
Positioned between the city's two famous piazzas, La Costa claims to be the oldest pizzeria in town. The non-pizza menu is limited, but excellent. Good service and in summer you can eat alfresco.
➕ 199 D2 ⊠ Piazza Bra 2
☎ 045 597468

Il Desco €€€
The grandest place in town, serving fine cooking in wonderful surroundings. Booking essential.
➕ 199 D2 ⊠ Via Dietro San Sebastiano 7 ☎ 045 595358
⊘ Closed Sun and Mon (but open Mon eve in Jul and Aug). Also closed for two weeks from Christmas and two weeks in early Jun

Il Dolmen €€
Stone archways here do indeed recall a neolithic burial chamber, although there is also a garden. Fish dishes a speciality. Long wine list.
➕ 199 D2 ⊠ Vicolo Cieco San Pietro Incarnario 5/7 ☎ 045 800745
⊘ Closed Mon

Greppia €€
Close to Via Cappello and Piazza Erbe in a quiet square. Veronese dishes and a great atmosphere.
➕ 199 D2 ⊠ Vicolo Samaritana 3c
☎ 045 8004577 ⊘ Closed Mon. Also closed for two weeks in Jan and Jun

Mondodoro €
Fine old osteria just off Via Mazzini offering year-round al fresco dining. Veronese menu and local wines.
➕ 199 D2 ⊠ Via Mondo d'Oro 4
☎ 045 8032679 ⊘ Closed Mon

Where to... Shop

Verona has all the shopping appeal to be expected of a major European city. And this being Italy, it excels in leather and fashion.

VIA MAZZINI

For general shopping, including fashions, shoes etc, the best place is Via Mazzini and the nearby streets. Via Mazzini itself is home to Gucci, Versace, Max Mara, Marinarinaldi, Bulgari and Cartier, among others. But there are also less internationally famous shops that are worth visiting.

For young fashion try **Promod**, **Pimkie** and **Oltre**. For shoes and bags look at **Rossetti**, **Bruschi** and **Furla**. **Erbovoglio** is excellent for children's clothes and shoes, while

Damiani has shirts and blouses. **Al Duca d'Aosta** has high-quality clothes and shoes for both men and women. A huge range of leather goods can be found at **Campana**, with everything from wallets to luggage.

Fiorucci and **Upim**, Verona's biggest department stores, are also in Via Mazzini (No 6 and No 10).

LEATHER

As well as the Via Mazzini shops try **Principe** (on the corner of Via Alberto Mario and Piazzetta Scalette Rubiani). There is also **Bettanin & Venturi** (Vicolo Morette 4) where shoes have been made for almost 150 years, and **Folli Follie** (Via Oberdan 9a/b) with shoes and bags.

FASHION

Corso Porta Borsari has many elegant fashion shops such as **Carlo Bottico** and **Just Cavalli** for women, while **Dismero** at No 53,

Patrizia Pepe and **iam** design for a younger, trendier clientele. Also of note are **Mariella Burani** at No 28 and **Stizzoli**, next door at No 30; both offer women classical elegance and something a little different.

For something more avant garde, go to **Lazzari** (Piazza Erbe 15). **Class Country** (Via San Rochetto 6) has traditional men's styles, as does **Class Uomo** at No 13b in the same street. **Camicissima** (Piazza Bra 3) has a large range of inexpensive men's shirts.

ANTIQUES

The best area for antiques is **Corso Sant'Anastasia** and the adjacent streets. There are also good shops closer to the Duomo. However, be cautious, as there is a thriving trade in reproductions.

ART GALLERIES

There are several very good art galleries around **Piazza Erbe**.

JEWELLERY

Damiani has an outlet at No 59 Via Mazzini and it is also worth visiting **G&G Amighini** (Piazzetta Monte 3), which specialises in silver.

OUT OF TOWN

North of Verona, in the Centro Commerciale at Affi, there is a warehouse outlet selling a wide range of Italian clothing and footwear.

MARKETS

There is a daily market in **Piazza Erbe**. There are also markets in **Piazza San Zeno** on Tuesdays and Fridays, in **Piazza Isolo** on Tuesdays and in **Piazza Santa Toscana** on Wednesdays and Fridays. Every third Saturday of the month there are antiques, objets d'art and crafts in **Piazza San Zeno**.

Where to...
Be Entertained

CARNIVAL

Verona carnival is one of the oldest in Italy, dating back to the early 16th century. It is held in the early spring. Contact the tourist office for exact times. The highlight of the event is the last Friday before Shrove Tuesday, known as the Bacchanal del Gnocchi, at which the Papa del Gnocco, holding a huge potato dumpling on a fork, takes charge.

FESTIVALS

There is an **international film festival** in the city in April. From June to August there are Shakespearean plays (performed in Italian) in the Roman Theatre.

At Christmas the **Festa di Santa Lucia** is held, with seasonal street markets in Piazza Bra and Via Roma. The Piazza Bra celebrations include displays of cribs from around the world in the arcades of the Arena.

The **Opera Festival** held in the Arena in July and August is world famous. Book ahead (tel: 045 8005151) to be sure of a ticket. Hotels can be busy too, so it is worth booking in advance.

THEATRE

As well as the Roman Theatre, there are several other theatres in the city. The **Teatro Nuovo** has a famous drama festival from December to April, while operas are staged at the **Teatro Filarmonico** from February to April.

NIGHTLIFE

The Veronese have their own version of a British 'pub-crawl' – *andar per goti*, 'going for a Gothic'. There are, consequently, a large number of bars, many of them with live music, particularly at the weekend. For the best, head for Piazza Bra or Piazza Erbe.

The city is surprisingly short of discos and nightclubs. Only the **Atlantis Pub** (Piazza Citadella 7) has regular live music, while **Alta Ego** (Via Torricelle) attracts a younger crowd.

There are, however, several out-of-town nightspots. **Berfei's Club** is a disco/restaurant (Via Lussemburgo 1) off the road towards the A4 *autostrada* (Verona Sud exit). Alternatively, try **Night City Club** (Via Bresciana 1f) which is located off the SS11 Verona–Peschiera road.

CHILDREN

The Arena offers the possibility of treading ground once trodden by gladiators, and Castelvecchio and its weaponry will also appeal to some children. The old defensive walls around the city have now been made into parkland and two of these have good play areas for children – **Arsenale** near Castelvecchio, and **Raggio di Sole** near Porta Nuovo.

The **Tropic del Sole**, close to Bussolengo, northwest of Verona, has a vast swimming pool with rock towers and other 'natural' features, and a roller-skating rink. Although it is not specifically aimed at children, most will enjoy it. Also at Bussolengo the **Parco Natura Viva** is a combination safari park and zoo. It includes a dinosaur park with life-size models.

Northern Lombardy

Getting Your Bearings

Sandwiched between Lake Como and Lake Garda is country comprising the edge of the Lombardy Plain and the foothills of the high Alps. Here there are two distinctly different towns, Bréscia and Bergamo, a fine lake and one of the most important valleys in Europe for prehistoric sites.

Bréscia is Lombardy's second city, a prosperous place with interesting Roman remains, some good Renaissance buildings and a museum housing some of the finest Lombard treasures in Italy. Yet it lacks a certain something – that it is difficult to put a finger on – which means that it is rarely on the itinerary of visitors to the lakes area. It is, perhaps, a little too big and so lacks the intimacy of Verona; or, perhaps, a little too modern, the bustle of the main streets distracting the visitor; or, perhaps, it is because it hides its treasures – they are tucked away so that you have to search for them and the search can be wearying.

Bergamo could not be more different. Here the modern town is laid out at the base of a hill. And at the top of the hill is old Bergamo, an almost complete and perfect Renaissance town. Its main sights are just a few minutes' walk apart and can be enjoyed in their unspoilt glory.

San Pellegrino Terme

Almenno San Salvatore

342

470

Ponte San Pietro

Bergamo **3**

Dalmine

591

Cologno al Serio

Fresco detail of the life of St Giúlia by Floriano Ferramola, in the Church of Santa Maria Solario

★ Don't Miss

At Your Leisure

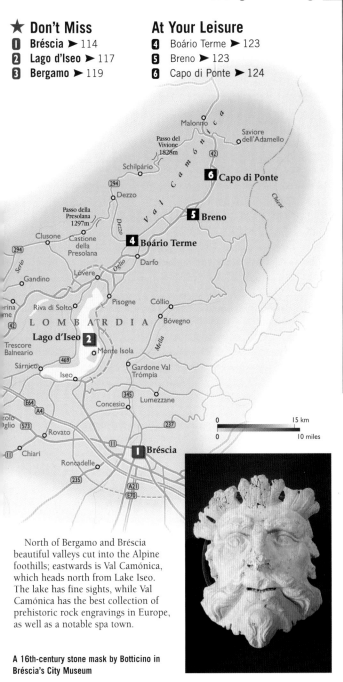

North of Bergamo and Bréscia beautiful valleys cut into the Alpine foothills; eastwards is Val Camónica, which heads north from Lake Iseo. The lake has fine sights, while Val Camónica has the best collection of prehistoric rock engravings in Europe, as well as a notable spa town.

A 16th-century stone mask by Botticino in Bréscia's City Museum

The two major towns of Northern Lombardy, Bréscia and Bergamo, are the focus of this drive, with a visit to Lake Iseo as a break from city streets.

Northern Lombardy In Three Days

Day One

Morning

Start your day in **3 Bergamo**'s Città Bassa (Lower City), saying hello to Donizetti outside the theatre named in his honour and having a look at the shops in the **Sentierone** (➤ 119). Next follow Via Roma/Via Vittorio Emanuele II to reach the cable-car to Città Alta (Upper City), the old town. Head straight up to Piazza Vecchia, then visit the Duomo, Santa Maria Maggiore and the **Colleoni Capella** (➤ 121). Have lunch in one of the restaurants in Piazza Vecchia – perhaps the Caffè de Tasso.

Afternoon

From Piazza Vecchia follow Via Gombito back towards the cable-car top station, but instead of riding down follow the road downhill past the Rocca, to your left, to reach an open area where you can view the old town walls and look north to the pre-Alps. Turn right through the Porta Sant'Agostino, an old gateway through the walls, and then bear left along Via di Noca to reach the **Accademia Carrara** (➤ 121). You can enjoy the rest of the afternoon working your way through the collection of paintings here.

Evening

In the evening walk back up into Piazza Vecchia (left) and have dinner in the Colleoni e dell'Angelo restaurant, which serves excellent food in a beautiful setting. By the time you have finished eating the square will be floodlit.

Day Two

Morning

Travel to **1 Bréscia**, arriving in the late morning. Start your exploration of the town in **Piazza della Vittoria** (➤ 114) with its Liberty architecture, then continue north to Piazza della Loggia to enjoy the medieval buildings.

You will probably want to have lunch here, and there are few better places in town.

Afternoon

Now take the passageway beneath the clock tower to reach Piazza Paolo VI and Bréscia's **twin cathedrals** (right, ➤ 115). It is worth visiting each for their art treasures. After your visit walk past the Broletto and turn right along Via dei Musei to see the best of the Roman remains – the Capitoline Temple – and to visit the town museum, with its Lombard treasures.

Evening

If you are staying the night in Bréscia rather than on Lake Iseo, take an early-evening stroll up onto the Colle Cidneo to enjoy the parkland and the views of the old fortress. Then head back down to the old town to enjoy a meal in one of Bréscia's excellent restaurants, perhaps La Sosta in Via San Martino della Battaglia.

Day Three

Morning

Make an early start and follow the eastern shore of **2 Lago d'Iseo** (➤ 117–118), taking the road along the Val Camónica from Pisogne to reach **4 Boário Terme** (➤ 123) in time for lunch, perhaps at the Airone at Via Nazionale 15.

Afternoon

After a quick exploration of the town, continue along the main valley road to reach **6 Capo di Ponte** (➤ 124), where you will want to explore some of the rock engravings on foot as well as visiting the museum.

Evening

How you spend the evening will depend on where you are staying the night. You can easily make it back to Bréscia, but if your destination is more local you might perhaps drive back to Lake Iseo and watch the sun go down behind the hills that mark its western shore.

⓪ Bréscia

With a population of around 195,000, Bréscia is Lombardy's second city after Milan. Famous in Italy for its steel-making, it is an industrial and commercial centre lacking the romantic appeal of Verona and Bergamo, which lie equidistant either side. For that reason it is often neglected by visitors to the Lake Garda area, yet it has important historical sites that are worth seeking out.

Piazza della Loggia

The middle of old Bréscia lay to the west of the cathedral, but in the 1930s the Fascist rulers of the city bulldozed the area to create the Piazza della Vittoria, a large but cheerless open space. A few steps north allows a comparison between the architecture of Renaissance Italy and that of Mussolini's less imaginative era.

In **Piazza della Loggia**, the loggia (also occasionally called the Palazzo Pubblico) is an exquisite late 15th- to early 16th-century building, combining sensual ground floor arches with a rather more formal first floor and an exuberant balustrade. Only the bulbous pale green roof – added in the 18th century after the original had been destroyed by fire – seems out of place. So exactly right are the dimensions of the building and its sculptured detail that it is no surprise to learn that two of

Clock face (above) of the Torre dell'Orologio and the loggia (below), both in the Piazza della Loggia

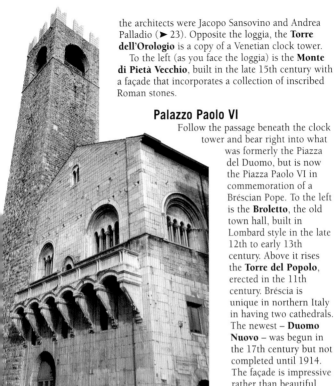

the architects were Jacopo Sansovino and Andrea Palladio (► 23). Opposite the loggia, the **Torre dell'Orologio** is a copy of a Venetian clock tower.

To the left (as you face the loggia) is the **Monte di Pietà Vecchio**, built in the late 15th century with a façade that incorporates a collection of inscribed Roman stones.

Palazzo Paolo VI

Follow the passage beneath the clock tower and bear right into what was formerly the Piazza del Duomo, but is now the Piazza Paolo VI in commemoration of a Bréscian Pope. To the left is the **Broletto**, the old town hall, built in Lombard style in the late 12th to early 13th century. Above it rises the **Torre del Popolo**, erected in the 11th century. Bréscia is unique in northern Italy in having two cathedrals. The newest – **Duomo Nuovo** – was begun in the 17th century but not completed until 1914. The façade is impressive rather than beautiful and hides the cathedral's

The Broletto, with the Torre del Popolo, Bréscia's oldest tower, behind it

elegant dome. Inside there is a 15th-century wooden crucifix, but nothing that compares to the treasures in the **Rotonda** (or Duomo Vecchio) next door. Built in the 11th century on the site of an earlier church (parts of which were incorporated) and Roman Bréscia's public baths, the old cathedral has an unusual circular Romanesque plan. Inside there are a great number of medieval treasures, including the red marble sarcophagus of Bishop Bernardo Maggi and, above the high altar, an Assumption by Maretto, arguably his masterpiece.

Roman Bréscia

Leave the square along the left side of the Broletto (Via dei Musei) crossing two roads to reach, after about 350m (382 yards), the heart of Roman Bréscia. Here stands the remains of the **Capitoline Temple** built in AD 73 by the Emperor Vespasian. Beside the temple, but largely unexcavated, is the Roman theatre. The narrow Piazza del Faro opposite the temple is the site of the Roman forum.

A little farther along Via dei Musei is a complex of buildings that began in 753 as a Benedictine nunnery raised by the Lombard King Desiderius' wife. Three separate churches were added later, the whole now comprising the **Museo della Città**, which houses several very important works. The bronze winged victory is 1st-century Roman; the 8th-century Cross of Desiderius includes over 200 jewels; while the ivory coffer is a 4th-century reliquary.

Castello e Pinacoteca

From Via dei Musei you have a choice; either head north to the Colle Cidneo (Cydnean Hill), or south to the city's art gallery in Via Martinengo da Barco. The Cydnean Hill formed an important part of Roman Bréscia. It is now dominated by a castle mainly built when the Viscontis ruled Bréscia. Today the castle houses the **Museo delle Armi Antichi 'Luigi Marzoli'** (Luigi Marzoli Museum of Antique Weapons), a collection of 15th- to 18th-century arms and armour. Below the museum the **Museo del Risorgimento** illustrates the struggle for Italian unification.

The **Pinacoteca Tosio–Martinengo** (Tosio-Martinengo Art Gallery), in a 16th-century palazzo, has works by Tintoretto, Moretto, Romanino and Giovanni Bellini, but the real treasures are two early works by Raphael, one of which, an Angel, is exquisite.

TAKING A BREAK

Coffea di Nevola Ivan, at Corso Zanardelli 26, serves great coffee and hot chocolate. For something more substantial try the **Raffa** at No 15 in nearby Corso Magenta.

Remnants of the Roman Capitoline Temple, lost beneath a land-slide and not rediscovered until 1823

➕ 198 A3
Museo della Città
✉ Via dei Musei 81b ☎ 030 2977833 🕐 Jun–Sep Tue–Sun 10–6; Oct–May Tue–Sun 9.30–5.30 💰 Expensive

Museo delle Armi Antichi 'Luigi Marzoli'
✉ Catello di Cidneo ☎ 030 293292 🕐 Jun–Sep Tue–Sun 10–6; Oct–May Tue–Sun 9.30–1, 2.30–5 💰 Moderate

Museo del Risorgimento
✉ Catello di Cidneo ☎ 030 44176 🕐 Jun–Sep Tue–Sun 10–5; Oct–May Tue–Sun 9.30–1, 2.30–5 💰 Moderate

Pinacoteca Tosio–Martinengo
✉ Via Martinengo da Barco 1 ☎ 030 3774999 🕐 Tue–Sun 10–1, 2–6 💰 Moderate

---

BRÉSCIA: INSIDE INFO

Top tip Bréscia is notoriously difficult for parking. If you are not staying in the city overnight, **try to arrive early and find a space in one of the big car parks** near Corso Zanardelli (the one in Piazza Vittoria is well signed) so as to be close to the tourist office and the main sights.

One to miss If time is short the **arms museum at the castle** is more interesting to the general visitor than the more specialist Risorgimento collection.

2 Lago d'Iseo

Lake Iseo is the fifth-largest of the northern lakes – 24km (15 miles) long and 5km (3 miles) across at its widest point. Monte Isola, roughly in the middle, is the longest lake island in Europe.

The Eastern Lake

If you arrive at the lake from Bréscia along the N510 you will have journeyed through the *corte franca* (free court). The origins of the name are disputed – is it from medieval times when this area of swampland was drained and claimed by monks whose 'courts' (holdings) were 'free' of taxes? Or is it much earlier, dating from the time of Charlemagne's conquest of the area? At Provaglio the Church of San Pietro in Lomosa was founded by Cluniac monks in 1083, evidence that the former explanation might be correct. The draining of the swamps failed at one resolutely wet area. Now called Le Torbiere, this peat bog is famed for its water-lilies, marsh plants and water-birds, and remnants of prehistoric pile dwellings have been found here.

The first place you will reach on the lake is the town of **Iseo**, an unashamed holiday resort but a good one. In the main square, Piazza Garibaldi, the great man's statue gazes moodily at you as you search out the 11th-century Church of Sant'Andrea to

The best view of the *bögns* is from a lake steamer as it nears Lóvere (above)

see the tomb of local lord Count Giacomo Oldofredi, which was added three centuries after the church's completion.

Now head north along the lake's eastern shore, with fine views of **Monte Isola**. On the summit is the **Church of the Madonna della Ceriola**, a place of pilgrimage for centuries. The island can be reached most easily from Sulzano, a sailing centre with a neat 15th-century church.

At Marone a road to the right leads to Zone (see Inside Info below). After the last tunnel the view across the water to the *bögns*, the huge sheets of limestone that plunge into the lake at Castro, is spectacular.

The Western Lake

At Pisogne the **Val Camónica** (▶ 123–124) branches off, but you will cross the inflowing Óglio to reach Lóvere, where the 19th-century Palazzo Tadini houses the **Galleria dell'Accademia Tadini** – small collections of art including works by Tiepolo and Bellini, porcelain and arms.

From Lóvere a narrow road edges nervously past the *bögns*, then widens to follow the western shore to Sárnico at the lake's tip. This neat little town has several villas built by Giuseppe Sommaruga (1867–1917), one of the better Italian art nouveau architects.

TAKING A BREAK

In Iseo the best options are in Piazza Garibaldi. For a meal try **Osteria Antico Melone**, which has a small menu of local specialities. At the northern end of the lake the best choice is a café in Pisogne's arcaded **Piazza del Mercato**.

➕ 197 F3
Galleria dell'Accademia Tadini
✉ Palazzo Tadini, Lóvere ☎ 035 960132 ◉ May–Oct Tue–Fri 3–7, Sat–Sun 10–12, 3–6;
Nov–Apr Sat–Sun 10–12, 3–6 💶 Moderate

LAGO D'ISEO: INSIDE INFO

Hidden gem On the road to Zone from Marone, on the eastern shore, just below the village of Cislano, look north to see the extraordinary **piramidi di erosione**. These spires of earthy conglomerate, some topped by huge boulders, were formed by glacial erosion.

❸ Bergamo

Bergamo is not one but two distinctly different cities.
Città Bassa, the Lower City, is late 19th- to early 20th-
century, laid out on a grand scale with a geometric array of
broad avenues. Perched on a hill above it is the Città Alta,
the Upper City, a haphazard jumble of streets and alleys
hemmed in by ancient walls.

Città Bassa

Piazza de
Liberata in the
Lower City

At the centre of Bergamo's Lower City is **Piazza Matteotti**, its
gardens split by Viale Roma which – changing names in both
directions – links the Upper City with the railway station. On
one side of Viale Roma, Piazza Matteotti leads to Via XX
Septembre, the city's main shopping street. On the other side
stands the **Teatro Donizetti**. Built in the 18th century to hold
1,300 people, the theatre was given a new façade and a new
name to celebrate the hundredth anniversary of the birth of
Bergamo's most famous son, the composer Gaetano Donizetti
(1797–1848). Beyond the theatre is Piazza Cavour, where
Donizetti is depicted listening thoughtfully to Melpomene
(the muse of song) as she plays her lyre.

Across from the theatre is the **Sentierone**, the 'Big Path',
which, with its cafés and shops, is a favourite with city
dwellers. The Sentierone forms part of Via Torquato Tasso. If
you love religious art, follow this away from the city centre to
see work by the Venetian Lorenzo Lotto (c1480–1556). His
altarpiece of the Madonna in the **Church of San Bartolomeo**

> **Curious Fact**
> The funicular to the Upper City is 240m (262 yards) long and rises by 82m
> (269ft). The left track is 6m (20ft) shorter than the right because of the curve. On
> 20 September, 1887, when the railway was officially opened, the first carriage
> was filled with local dignitaries eager to take their place in history. Sadly, a wheel
> on the carriage jammed and the illustrious group had to walk back down the track.

(to the left) is one of his masterpieces and there are other
works in the churches of San Spirito and San Bernardino
farther along the road.

Città Alta

Despite the Lower City's elegance, you will soon be anxious to
head for the Upper City. There is only one way to do this –
follow Viale Roma, which becomes Via Vittorio Emanuele II,
to the lower station of the funicular railway. In one sense this
is a short ride, but in another it is the opposite. You climb on
board and a few minutes later you have gone back 500 years
in time, to a hilltop city of Renaissance Italy where all but
essential vehicles are excluded.

From the funicular's top station cross the small square and
take narrow, winding Via Gombito uphill, passing the square,
stark 12th-century Torre Gombito to reach **Piazza Vecchia**,
one of the most enchanting squares in northern Italy. To your
right as you enter is the **Palazzo Nuovo**, designed by the
celebrated Renaissance architect Vicenzo Scamozzi
(1552–1616) and modelled on the Sansovino library in
Venice, and which also houses an important library.

To the left, at the centre of the square, is the **Contarini
Fountain**, presented to the town by Alvese Contarini, its
Venetian *podestà* (mayor), in 1780. Its lions, symbols of the
Venetian Republic, politely hold chains in their mouths. Only
16 years later the inhabitants of Bergamo decided the chains
of Venice were too much to bear and they tore the Venetian
lion from the façade of Torre Civica.

The **Palazzo della Ragione** dominates the opposite side of
the square from Palazzo Nuovo. It was rebuilt in the 16th
century after fire had
destroyed its predecessor.
The statue beside its central
portico is of the poet
Torquato Tasso (1544–95).
Beside the palazzo rises the
Torre Civica, the old city's
campanile, begun in the 11th
century, but not completed
for 400 years.

Go through the arched
passage beside the tower –
the covered stairway to your
right is the entrance to
Palazzo della Ragione – to
reach Piazza del Duomo. The

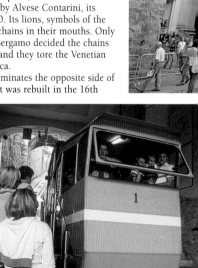

Duomo is so hemmed in by other buildings that it is difficult to gain a complete view. It has a fine dome, a late baroque façade and, inside, several fine works of art, including *The Martyrdom of St John* by Tiepolo and bronze angels by Antonio Fontana.

But despite being the city's cathedral, the Duomo is outshone by the **Church of Santa Maria Maggiore,** beside it. Raised in the 12th century by a city exhausted by war, plague and drought, and in need of spiritual assistance, it is plain on the outside, but vast and sumptuous inside. Built into the church is the **Colleoni Capella,** which is even more majestically decorated. It was designed by Giovanni Antonio Amadeo for Bartolomeo Colleoni (► 22). Next to Santa Maria Maggiore is the 14th-century polygonal baptistery, which originally stood inside the church but was taken down and reconstructed in its present position some 200 years ago.

Below: the ornate Colleoni Chapel. Colleoni's tomb, and that of his daughter, lie inside

From Piazza del Duomo it is best to wander the old streets at random. Music lovers may want to see the **birthplace of Donizetti** at 14 Via Borgo Canale, or the museum to him at 9 Via Arena, while nature lovers will seek out the **Museo de Scienze Naturali e Caffi** (Natural History Museum). It is housed in the 14th-century Visconti Cittadella along with the **Museo Civico Archeologico** (Archaeology Museum).

But most famous of all is the **Galleria dell' Accademia Carrara**. It is reached from the Città Alta by going through Porta San Agostino (the road entrance at the eastern end) then turning left down a cobbled path, or from the Lower City along Via Verdi, Via S Giovanni and Via Battisti. The gallery – founded in 1796 by Count Giacomo Carrara – has works by Raphael, Titian, Botticelli, Rubens and Mantegna, among others, making it one of the best galleries in northern Italy. Opposite is the **Galleria d'Arte Moderna e Contemporanea** (Museum of Modern and Contemporary Art).

Left: the funicular links the Upper and Lower cities

TAKING A BREAK

This really depends on where you are. In the Upper City head for **Caffè de Tasso** in Piazza Vecchia; if you are in the Lower City then the **Balzer** at Portici Sentierone 41 has excellent snacks and coffee.

🔢 197 E3

Torre Civica
☎ 035 242226 🕐 Apr–Oct Tue–Sun 9.30–7 (9.30pm on Sat and public hols); Nov–Mar Sat and public hols 9.30–4.30 (at other times by request, but for groups of at least 5 people) 💷 Moderate

Colleoni Capella
☎ 035 210061 🕐 Mar–Oct Tue–Sun 9–12.30, 2–6.30; Nov–Feb Tue–Sun 9–12.30, 2–4.30
💷 Free

Donizetti's Birthplace
☎ 035 247116 🕐 Jun–Sep Tue–Sun 9.30–1, 2–5.30; Oct–May Tue–Fri 9.30–1, Sat and public hols 9.30–1, 2–5.30

Museo Donizettiano
✉ Via Arena 9 ☎ 035 399269 🕐 Jun–Sep Tue–Sun 9.30–1, 2–5.30; Oct–May 9.30–1, Sat–Sun 9.30–1, 2–4.30 💷 Inexpensive

Museo de Scienze Naturali e Caffi
✉ Piazza Citadella 10 ☎ 035 399422 🕐 Apr–Sep Tue–Fri 9–12.30, 2.30–6, Sat–Sun 9–7; Oct–Mar Tue–Sun 9–12.30, 2.30–5.30 💷 Free

Museo Civico Archeologico
✉ Piazza Citadella 10 ☎ 035 242839 🕐 Apr–Sep Tue–Fri 9–12.30, 2.30–6, Sat–Sun 9–7; Oct–Mar Tue–Sun 9–12.30, 2.30–6 💷 Free

Accademia Carrara
✉ Piazza Carrara 82a ☎ 035 399677 🕐 Tue–Sun 10–1, 3–6.45 💷 Moderate (free entry on Sun) ❓ No photography

Galleria d'Arte Moderna e Contemporanea
✉ Via San Tomaso 53 ☎ 035 399528 🕐 Apr–Sep Tue–Sun 10–1, 3–6.45; Oct–Mar Tue–Sun 9.30–1, 2.30–5.45 💷 Free (except when there is an exhibition)

Children playing by the Contarini Fountain in Piazza Vecchia, Bergamo

BERGAMO: INSIDE INFO

Hidden gem In **Piazza Mercato del Fieno**, opposite the Torre Gombito in Bergamo's Città Alta, there is a pair of medieval tower-houses, one six storeys high, the other four storeys.

At Your Leisure

4 Boário Terme

The town is named for the natural hot water which is piped to the Thermal Establishment, a fine building set among gardens and parkland and with a backdrop of high peaks. Two centuries or so ago visits to spas were part of the social scene of the rich and leisured, and towns such as Boário sprang up all over Europe. When society moved on, the use of mineral waters continued.

Today Boário's water is famed for its curative properties for liver and intestinal problems, its successes having made it the third most important spa in Italy. The town's 40-odd hotels testify to the prosperity brought by the water, which is also bottled.

Close to Boário in the **Parco delle Luine** are the first of the rock carvings for which the Val Camónica is renowned. Alternatively, follow the road into the Val di Scalve, going through Ángolo Terme, a small spa village. From here a narrow road reaches the deep-blue **Lago Moro**, while the main road cuts through the Dezzo Gorge for fine views of the Oróbie Alps.

➕ 198 A4
Parco delle Luine
☎ 348 7374467 ⏰ Tue–Sun 9–12, 2–6 (5pm Oct–Mar) 👊 Free

5 Breno

From Boário Terme the road through the Val Camónica heads towards Breno, but a short detour leads to Ésine, where the 14th-century **Church of Santa Maria Assunta** is

Rock carvings in the Val Camónica

Breno, with Adamello Mountain behind

a National Monument for its campanile and 15th-century frescoes. Cividate Camuno is named for its position as the Roman capital of the valley. Breno is the modern 'capital', a neat town dominated by a gloomy 14th-century castle with under-ground dungeons. The town's museum explores local history and has paintings by local artists.

➕ 198 B4

Castello

☎ 0364 22970 🕐 Daily 9am–10pm
🎫 Free

Museo

🕐 Closed for restoration at the time of writing. Tel: 0364 22041 for details

🟢 Capo di Ponte

Val Camónica became famous when the first engravings into the soft local Permian sandstone were discovered a century or so ago. Today about 200,000 images of animals and people have been discovered, ranging from neolithic to Roman times, but chiefly from the time of Iron Age Camuni people. Since 1979 their importance has been recognised by UNESCO, who have declared it a world heritage site.

At Capo di Ponte, about 12km (7 miles) north of Breno, a museum is devoted to the carvings and there is a study centre. Here, too, is the **Parco Nazionale delle Incisioni Rupestri**, a national park set up to protect the engravings. These include hunting scenes, warriors, horsemen, carts, huts and shaman figures. Among the better examples are the 1,000 or so engravings on the Naquane rock. There are also two large decorated rocks near Cemmo, where there is the oldest representa-tion of a cart so far discovered. It is, perhaps, 5,000 years old. The nearby **Museo Didatico d'Arte e Vita Preistorico** has a reconstructed Camuni village.

➕ 198 B5

Centro Camuno di Studi Preistorico

✉ Capo di Ponte ☎ 0364 42091
🕐 Mon–Fri 9–5 🎫 Free

Parco Nazionale delle Incisioni Rupestri

☎ 0364 42140 🕐 Tue–Sun 8.30–7.30
(4.30pm Oct–Apr) 🎫 Moderate

Museo Didatico d'Arte e Vita Preistorico

✉ Cemmo ☎ 0364 42148
🕐 Jun–Sep daily 8.30–12.30, 1.30–6
(5.30pm rest of year) 🎫 Free

Where to... Stay

Prices

Expect to pay per double room, per night

€ under €70   €€ €70–€130   €€€ over €130

BERGAMO

Agnello d'Oro €€

Set in the Upper City, the building dates from the late 16th century. Some bedrooms overlook the small square in front. Simply furnished but comfortable rooms.

✚ 197 E3 ⊠ Via Gombito 22
☎ 035 249883; fax: 035 235612

Cappello d'Oro €€€

A Best Western Premier hotel at the heart of the Lower City. Bedrooms are relatively small, but well decorated and furnished. Private car park and an excellent restaurant.

✚ 197 E3 ⊠ Viale Papa Giovanni XXIII ☎ 035 232503;
www.hotelcappellodoro.it

Città dei Mille €

This is an inexpensive hotel on the road to the *autostrada*, but about a 30-minute walk – or a bus ride – from the Lower City's centre. Bedrooms are on floors of different colours and the hotel has memorabilia from Garibaldi's force (➤ 23).

✚ 197 E3 ⊠ Via Autostrada 3c
☎ 035 317400; email:
reservation@cittadiemille.it

Excelsior San Marco €€€

Midway between the funicular to the Upper City and the Lower City centre. Spacious rooms, some with a view of the Upper City. The hotel restaurant (the Colonna) is one of the best in the city. Private car park.

✚ 197 E3 ⊠ Piazza della Repubblica 6 ☎ 035 366111;
www.hotelsanmarco.com

BOÀRIO TERME

Rizzi €€€

One of the best hotels in a spa town where there is a lot of competition. Spacious, well-appointed rooms. The spa itself is just 100m (109 yards) away should you wish to try. A lovely garden and a very good restaurant.

✚ 198 A4 ⊠ Via Carducci 11
☎ 0364 531617; www.albergorizzi.it

BRENO

Giardino €

Ideally sited for an exploration of Val Camonica, this medium-size hotel has good facilities.

✚ 198 B4 ⊠ Via 28 Aprile
☎ 0364 321184;
www.cominelli.com/hotelgiardino

BRÉSCIA

Albergo Orologio €€

Recently renovated, this small boutique hotel is just behind Piazza Loggia. Ask for a room with a view. Care has been taken to blend antique furniture with modern amenities. The staff are very friendly and helpful.

✚ 198 A3 ⊠ Via Beccaria 17
☎ 030 375411;
www.albergoorologio.it

Trento €

This small hotel is within walking distance of all the main visitor sights and the shopping centre. Pleasant rooms, a good restaurant and friendly staff.

✚ 198 A3 ⊠ Piazza Cesari Battisti 27–29 ☎ 030 380768; fax: 030 3387987

Where to...
Eat and Drink

Prices
Expect to pay for a three-course meal for one, excluding drinks and service
€ under €30   **€€** €30–€60   **€€€** over €60

BERGAMO

Airoldi €
A solid option for light lunches, dinners and drinks in the Lower Town. Daily chalkboard items include steaks and pastas.
+ 197 E3 **✉** Viale Papa Giovanni XXIII 18 **☎** 035 244 423 **◉** Mon–Sat 7 am–11 pm

Borgo €
Lively, colourful osteria packed with locals enjoying good home cooking. A wood-burning oven bakes the pizzas and a wider menu for €25 is offered in the evening.
+ 197 E3 **✉** Via San Lazzaro 8 **☎** 035 242452 **◉** Closed Sun

La Bruschetta €€
A beautiful building with arched stone ceilings. Fish and meat dishes and an excellent range of pizzas.
+ 197 E3 **✉** Via G d'Alzano 1 **☎** 035 221265 **◉** Closed Mon. Dinner only

Colleoni & Dell'Angelo €€€
Housed in a medieval palazzo with arched ceilings and frescoed walls. The Bergamesque ravioli with butter and sage is hard to beat.
+ 197 E3 **✉** Piazza Vecchia 7 **☎** 035 232596 **◉** Closed Mon and for two weeks in Aug

Da Ornella €€
Lovely little place in the old town specialising in polenta served with meat in cast-iron bowls. Also polenta taragna (ie cooked with butter and cheese) and rabbit.
+ 197 E3 **✉** Via Gombito 15 **☎** 035 232736 **◉** Closed Thu and Fri lunch

BOÁRIO TERME

Airone €
The pizzocheri and polenta, and a stew of beef shin with porcini mushrooms and cream, are the highlights here, but there is much else to enjoy in this charming restaurant.
+ 198 A4 **✉** Via Nazionale 15 **☎** 0364 531276

BRÉSCIA

Al Teatro €
Excellent pizzeria close to the city centre. Good menu and value-for-money pizzas.
+ 198 A3 **✉** Via Mazzini 36 **☎** 030 44251 **◉** Closed Mon and Tue lunch and Sun

Castello Malvezzi €€
Elegant building with good ambience. Traditional dishes with a twist, including smoked horse meat, which is delicious.
+ 198 A3 **✉** Via Colle San Giuseppe **☎** 030 2004224 **◉** Closed Mon and Tue. Dinner only Wed–Fri

La Sosta €€
A marvellous restaurant in the 17th-century stables of the Palazzo Martinengo. Brescian specialities such as goat are on the menu. Booking in advance is advised.
+ 198 A3 **✉** Via San Martino della Battaglia 20 **☎** 030 295603 **◉** Closed Mon and Sun eve

Where to... Shop

As major cities both Bréscia and Bergamo have large shopping areas and some out-of-town shopping. Many international names have shops in the two towns but some names will be unfamiliar to non-Italians.

BRÉSCIA

For jewellery the following are certainly worth a look: **Giarin** (Corso Magenta 8); try **Ghidini** (Corso Magenta 8b) for unusual, exciting designs; **Metalli** (Corso Palestro 38a); and **Emozioni d'Oro**, (Via Valcamonica 17) which sells silver, despite the name.

For shoes try **Fratelli Rossetti** (Corso Zanardelli 10); **Maison al Duomo** (Via IV Novembre 1a) for ladies' shoes only; and **Romano** (Corso Palestro13).

Many designer fabrics can be found at **Casa Sovrana** in Portici X Giornate.

And for antiques look out for **Cronos**, Galleria al Duomo (Via X Giornate); **Ceralacca** (Via Fratelli Porcellana 42); **Antic Oro** (Vicolo della Speranza 3d), for both old and new jewellery; and **Rino Fossati** (Via Beccaria 3a).

The biggest department store in the city centre is **Coin** at the corner of Corso Magenta and Via San Martino della Battaglia.

BERGAMO CITTÀ BASSA

There are many outlets for ladies' fashion in Via XX Septembre. For men's shirts try **Stelio** (Sentierone 46) and **Baggi** (Via XX Septembre 62–64). Inexpensive men's and women's clothes can be found at **Ciocca** (Via XX Septembre 20). **La Perla** (Sentierone 40) has high quality swimwear and underclothes.

For shoes look for **Pompeo** (Via XX Septembre 27); **Bruschi** (Via XX Septembre 39); **Fratelli Rossetti** (Via XX Septembre 52); and **Dev** (Via XX Septembre 85–87).

For handbags and other leather goods there is **Diana** (Via XX Septembre 40).

The area around the **Accademia Carrara** is popular with artists and there are several studios, most notably that of Sergio Garau (Via S Tomaso 88a), who paints onto old wood cloth. Close to Sergio's studio there is a good antique shop – **GLA Antichità** (Via S Tomaso 90).

The biggest department store in the city centre is **Coin** (Largo Medaglie d'Oro).

Out of town, to the northwest of Bréscia, the best place to head for is the **Franciacorta Outlet Village** (Rodengo Saiano): take the Ospitaletto exit from the *autostrada* A4. Here you will find 55 shops, including some designer names, as well as several cafés and restaurants.

BERGAMO CITTÀ ALTA

The Upper City is both much smaller and much more given over to outlets for visitors with its restaurants, bars etc. But there are some gems, including **Babilonia** (Via Gombito 12d), which sells chic ladies' clothing, while opposite the Colleoni restaurant in Piazza Vecchia is the shop of **Daniela Gregis** who designs and makes one-off articles.

For menswear **Franco Loda** (Via Gombito 17) is excellent, while **Cesare Albert** (Via Bartolomeo Colleoni 5b) is the place to go for some of the best children's clothes in the area.

Brivio (Via B Colleoni 19a) has excellent jewellery and silver. For gifts, the candles at **RR Candele** (Via B Colleoni 15m) are excellent value.

Cooperativa Libraria Il Quartiere (Via Gombito 24a) is a well-stocked stationers with a good range of special toys.

Where to...
Be Entertained

WALKING

Both Bergamo and Bréscia are excellent centres from which to explore the valleys that head north towards the Alps. North of Bergamo are the **Val Brembana** and **Val Seriana**. Val Seriana is famous for the Cascata del Serio (► 21).

North of Bréscia, there is fine country and fine walking in **Val Camónica**, **Val Sabbia** and **Val Trompia**, as well as in the **Franciacorta**, northwest of the city.

GOLF

There are several golf courses in the area close to Bergamo and Bréscia, though many have a limited number of holes. By common consent the best local course is the **Franciacorta**, near Rovato, close to the southern tip of Lake Iseo, which is an 18-hole, par 72 course.

OTHER SPORTS

There are opportunities for tennis, squash etc in the sports centres in each of the cities. From Bréscia, the watersports facilities on western Lake Garda can be comfortably reached (► 64).

THEATRE AND CINEMA

There are cinemas in Bréscia and Bergamo. At **Manérbio** – just off the A21 *autostrada* south of Bréscia – there is a multi-screen cinema. The **Donizetti Theatre** in Bergamo has four seasons each year. The opera season is from September to December; the drama season is from November to April. There is a jazz festival in February, and a season of dance/ballet from January to April.

The **Teatro Grande** in Bréscia has an opera season from September to November, a drama season from November to April and a season of concerts from October to March.

Bréscia also has two other theatres, **Teatro di Santa Chiara** and **Teatro Sancarlino**.

NIGHTLIFE

In Bergamo there are discos in Via Dalmine 10a Curno (**Clubbing**) and Via Bascensis (the **Ritmo**). There are also around a dozen discos and nightclubs in Bréscia. At present the popular ones are **Orange Blue** (146 Via Mandolossa), **Circus** (127 Via Dalmazia), and **Fura** (Via Lavagrome 13, Lonato).

FESTIVALS

Bréscia hosts an international **piano festival** (held jointly with Bergamo) from April to June and a series of organ concerts from mid-September to mid-October in city churches. Most famous of all is the **Mille Miglia** car race which, starting in Bréscia, was held annually until 1957, when it was stopped after a series of accidents involving the deaths of spectators. In 1977 the event was revived as a three-day veteran car rally in May from Bréscia to Ferrara, then to Rome and back to Bréscia.

MARKETS

There is an **antiques market** in Piazza Citadella in Bergamo's Città Alta on the third Sunday of the month. There is also a **book fair** at the Sentierone in April and May.

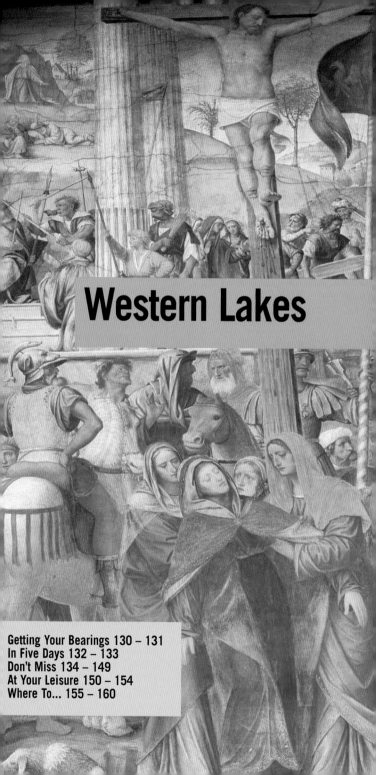

Western Lakes

Getting Your Bearings

To the west of Lake Garda there are four other lakes, each with its own character: Lake Orta is in a mountain hollow; Lake Maggiore is shared between two Italian provinces and has its northern tip in Switzerland; Lake Lugano is almost entirely within Switzerland; and Lake Como is famous for its villas and gardens.

The most westerly of the lakes is Lake Orta, which lies entirely within the region of Piemonte. At its southern end is the magical island of San Giúlio, where the saint of the name lies buried. You reach it from Orta San Giúlio, the most picturesque and interesting of the lake's towns.

Lake Orta drains into Lake Maggiore, famous for its group of three Borromean Islands. One of these, Isola Pescatori, is still much as it has been for

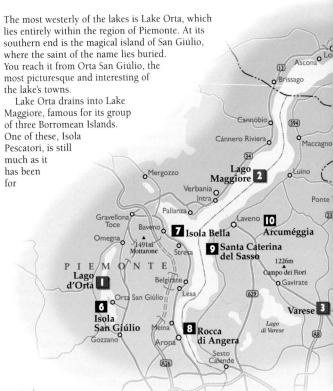

centuries,
but the others have been transformed by the Borromean family – Isola Madre into a beautiful park surrounding an elegant villa, Isola Bella into an extravaganza of villa and gardens.

Lake Lugano lies mainly in Switzerland, a journey around it crossing and recrossing the borders between the two countries. The city that shares the lake's name is the largest on the western lakes, modern, sophisticated and prosperous. That prosperity is mirrored at Campione d'Italia, the curious

Previous page:
A fresco
showing the
Crucifixion of
Christ in the
Church of Santa
Maria degli
Angioli, Lugano

★ Don't Miss

At Your Leisure

enclave that remains resolutely Italian, despite embracing Swiss systems.

Lake Como is the most elegant of the western lakes, its long shoreline dotted with stylish villas set in parkland. Here you can have your pick of high-quality hotels and restaurants, while on the ridges above Lake Lecco (the southern prong of Lake Como) you can walk off excellent meals.

This drive assumes you have spent the night in Orta
San Giúlio on Lake Orta.

In Five Days

Day 1

Morning/Lunch

After breakfast, take the short boat ride
to **6** **Isola San Giúlio** (➤ 150) to explore
the island and the Church of San Giúlio.
Return to **Orta San Giúlio** (➤ 135) and
drive along the eastern lakeside to
Omegna (➤ 135). Take the road towards
Domodossola, turning right at Mergozzo
to Lake Maggiore. Turn right (south)
beside it to reach **Stresa** (➤ 138–139).
Lunch at Stresa.

Afternoon/Evening

Cross to **7** **Isola Bella** (➤ 150) and tour
the extraordinary Borromean villa, then
take a quick stroll around the gardens
before taking the boat to **Isola Madre**
(right, ➤ 139–140) to enjoy the contrast
its 'subdued' villa and natural parkland
offer. Finally take the boat to **Isola
Pescatori** (➤ 139) for a walk through the
old streets and a coffee at the harbour,
before returning to Stresa for dinner.
Stay the night in Stresa.

Day 2

Morning/Lunch

Make an early start, driving south along the western shore to Arona, then
rounding the southern tip of the lake to reach **8** **Rocca di Angera** (➤ 151).
After your visit, continue north to reach **9** **Santa Caterina del Sasso**
(➤ 151). From the car park above the church it is a short drive
to Laveno, where you can have lunch.

Afternoon

Take the ferry from Laveno to Intra, heading north from there to Cánnero
Riviera and **Cannóbio** (➤ 138) and on to **Locarno** (➤ 137), stopping for
coffee in Piazza Grande. From Locarno follow the eastern shore southwards
to **Luino** (➤ 140), then head inland on the road to Ponte Tresa. Follow the
lakeside road through Porto Ceresio and into Switzerland to reach
Capolago. Turn left here to reach **12** **Campione d'Italia** (➤ 152).

Evening
Have dinner at Da Candida before enjoying the view across the lake to Lugano. Stay the night in Campione d'Italia.

Day 3

Morning
Take the first boat to **Lugano** (➤ 143) and enjoy a morning in the city.

Lunch
Return to Campione and drive to Ponte Chiasso. Cross into Italy and take the road to **Cernobbio** (➤ 147) for lunch.

Afternoon
Drive north along the western shore to **14 Villa Carlotta** (➤ 153). Visit the villa and gardens then take the ferry to Varenna to see **Villa Monastero** (➤ 148), and then another ferry to **15 Bellágio** (➤ 154).

Evening
After exploring the town have dinner at the **Bilacus** (➤ 157, booking needed) and stay the night in Bellágio.

Day 4

Morning/Lunch
Cross the lake again by ferry and drive south to Lenno for the boat to **13 Villa del Balbianello** (left, ➤ 153), continuing into Argegno for lunch.

Afternoon/Evening
After lunch, continue to **Como** (➤ 146–147), exploring the city and museum. Have dinner and stay the night in Como (➤ 155 and 157).

Day 5

Morning
Set off in the direction of **9 Varese** (➤ 141–142), stopping on the way at Castiglione Olona to visit the **Palazzo Branda Museo** and **Museo della Collegiata** (➤ 142). Continue to Varese where you can wander around the old town and visit the Palazzo Estense before stopping for lunch.

Afternoon
Drive to **Sacro Monte** and the **Monte Campo dei Fiori** (➤ 142) and end the day at the village of **10 Arcuméggia** (➤ 152).

▮ Lago d'Orta

Lake Orta, just 13.5km (8 miles) long and 2.5km (1.5 miles) wide at its widest point, the smallest of the great lakes, is also the westernmost, perched high in the mountains above Lake Maggiore. Its outflowing river, La Nigoglia, leaves Lake Orta at Omegna to join the Strona River, which flows down to reach the Toce River and Lake Maggiore.

La Nigoglia flows almost due north, towards the Alps, the only river in Italy which does so. This fact is said to be the basis of the independent attitude of Lake Orta's folk, a local saying maintaining that 'La Nigoglia flows up and we make the laws'.

Lakeside viewpoints offer a romantic setting

Close to the lake's southern tip is the town of **Gozzano**, where one church is dedicated to San Giuliano, while another (San Lorenzo) houses what is claimed to be the sarcophagus of the saint. San Giuliano was the brother of San Giúlio. When Giuliano stopped at Gozzano during their missionary pilgrimage his brother moved on to the lake, where the townsfolk of Orta asked for help in defeating the monsters, dragons and snakes that inhabited the offshore island. Giúlio threw his cloak on the water, stepped on it and, using his staff as a rudder, crossed to the island, vanquished the monsters and set up a hermit's cell where he lived for the rest of his life. The island is still called **Isola San Giúlio** (➤ 150) and the mainland town is now Orta San Giúlio.

Orta San Giúlio

Orta San Giúlio has a delightful lakeside square (Piazza Motta). Here the 16th-century Palazzo della Comunità, once the town hall, is frescoed, as are other houses in the tangle of steep, narrow streets that lead away from the square. One such is **Casa Morgarini** (House of Dwarves): the reason for the name is lost in time.

Above the town is the city's **Sacro Monte**, reached by a path threading its way through pine and beech woods. Along the way are 21 mainly 17th-century chapels with 376 terracotta statues illustrating the life of St Francis of Assisi, and almost 1,000 frescoes.

In the many chapels at Sacro Monte, life-size statues are dedicated to St Francis

The Northern Lake

From Orta San Giúlio a road follows the course of the lake's shoreline to reach **Omegna**, a small industrial town with fine old buildings and great viewpoints of the lake. At Quarna

Cobbled streets in Orta San Giúlio lead down to the water's edge

Sotto, near Omegna, there is a delightful small museum dedicated to musical instruments, the **Museo Etnografico e dello Strumento Musicale a Fiato**, the making of woodwind instruments having been a local craft for two centuries.

On the western side there is no lakeside road, and instead tight, meandering roads link pretty mountain villages and finally reach the **Church of Madonna del Sasso**, built in the 18th century. From here there is the very best view of the lake.

TAKING A BREAK

The cafés in Orta San Giúlio's Piazza Motta offer great coffee and superb views of the lake. For a meal **Venus** (tel: 0322 90362), also in Piazza Motta and right at the lakeside, is ideal for a leisurely lunch.

➕ 196 A4
Sacro Monte
🚶 Walk: open daily 24 hours. Chapels: May–Sep daily 9–7; Oct–Apr 9–4.30

Museo Etnografico e dello Strumento Musicale a Fiato (Museum of Musical Instruments)
✉ Quarna Sotto ☎ 0323 826368 🕐 15 Jun–15 Sep (or by request) Tue–Sun 10–12, 3–7
🎟 Moderate

The 17th-century church at Orta San Giúlio is worth the climb up the stepped Motta

LAGO D'ORTA: INSIDE INFO

Top tip At night, both Isola San Giúlio and the Church of Madonna del Sasso are **illuminated**.
• Very early in the morning a thin mist usually covers the lake and **Isola San Giúlio** appears to float on it – a magical sight.

2 Lago Maggiore

In his 1839 book *The Memoirs of a Tourist* French novelist Stendhal wrote: 'When a man has a heart and a shirt he should sell the shirt in order to see Lake Maggiore'.

Despite its name, Lake Maggiore is not the largest lake – that being Lake Garda – but it is the longest and has a 170km (105-mile) shoreline. The lake's northern tip lies in the Swiss canton of Ticino, its western shore in the Italian region of Piemonte, the eastern shore in Lombardy.

Locarno

Locarno, the largest town on the lake, has a distinctly Swiss veneer over its Italian style – that touch of efficient, punctual zeal. But the town wears it well, blending immaculate gardens and a marvellous tree-lined lake promenade with the more laid-back, Italianate pavement cafés and arcaded shops of Piazza Grande. Close to the piazza is the **Castello Visconti**, built by 15th-century Milanese lords. It now houses a museum of local history. One section deals with the 1925 Pact of Locarno, a valiant attempt to undo the worst excesses of the Treaty of Versailles that ultimately failed to bring Europe the peace it sought. From close to the town's railway station a cable-car rises to the 15th-century **Church of Madonna del Sasso**, built on the site of a vision of the Madonna. Inside is an altarpiece by Bramantino of the Flight into Egypt.

The formal gardens beside the lake are a refreshing place to stop and enjoy the view

Head south along the lake's western shore, passing **Ascona**, a town with a long artistic tradition. Swiss artist Paul Klee, novelist and poet Hermann Hesse and American dancer Isadora Duncan all spent time here – as did Lenin and Jung.

The Western Shore to Stresa

Continuing south the border is soon crossed, the first Italian town being **Cannóbio**, where a *pietà* in a local house was reputed to have shed real blood in 1522, a prelude to the town's escape from the devastations of the plague. The double miracle, and others which followed, caused a church to be built where the miraculous *pietà* was hung in a silver frame: almost immediately Cannóbio was again spared in another outbreak of plague.

From the town a great drive follows Val Cannóbina to Santa Maria Maggiore, and through the marvellous Centovalli (the Hundred Valleys) to Re, where the vast church houses another miraculous painting.

Beyond Cannóbio the ruined Malpaga castles are seen offshore. They were once occupied by pirates who preyed on lake traffic, until the Viscontis defeated them. Next comes Cánnero Riviera, the 'Nice of Maggiore', a town renowned for its winter climate. Southward, **Verbania**, as the collection of three towns – Intra, Pallanza and Verbania – is known, is a terminus for the lake's car ferry (to Laveno) and is the site of Maggiore's finest mainland garden, that of the **Villa Taranto**. This was the vision of a Scot, Neil McEacharn (a descendant of the Duke of Taranto, one of Napoleon's generals). The gardens cover 16ha (939 acres), are criss-crossed by 8km (5 miles) of path and have over 20,000 varieties of trees, shrubs and flowers. The gardens are open to the public, but not the villa.

The lake now throws an arm towards the Ossola Valley, the high Alps and Switzerland. To the south, beyond Baveno – where the Casa Morandi is an Italian National Monument and probably the most frequently photographed house on the lake – is Stresa, the most famous of Maggiore's towns.

Stresa and the Îles Borromées

Stresa's fame is based on its offshore islands and the annual music festival because, though pretty enough, particularly in Piazza Cadorna, Stresa has little to offer other than a row of upmarket hotels. One of these is the **Grand Hotel des Îles Borromées**, the only 5-star hotel on the lake. Of the three Borromean Islands, **Isola Bella** (▶ 150–151) is the most famous, but the

other, less exuberant, islands are, in their way, its equal. **Isola Pescatori** is still occupied by fisherfolk – you will see nets drying in the sun – and has a maze of narrow, shadowy alleys. **Isola Madre**, the largest of the three, has a fine 18th-century villa set in lovely parkland. After the lavishness of Isola Bella, Madre's understated beauty is the perfect antidote.

About 3km (2 miles) north of Stresa, in Piazzale Lido, a cable-car will whisk you to the top of **Monte Mottarone** for an exhilarating view of Monte Rosa. You can also admire the villa and the animal collection of **Villa Pallavicino**.

The Southeastern Lake

South of Villa Pallavicino the road hugs the lake shore, a signed turn right leading to the statue of San Carlo Borromeo before reaching Arona. From this busy town there is a great view across the lake to Angera Castle. At the southern end of the lake is Sesto Calende – Sesto C on all the road signs: the curious name dates from Roman times when a market was held here six days after *calends*, the first day of a new month.

The elegant waterside buildings in Pallanza are testament to the town's 19th-century popularity

The Eastern Lake

North of Sesto C is **Angera**, famous for its castle (➤ 151). The lake road now heads inland, bypassing the prominent broad headland of Ranco, to reach Ispra, where there is a European centre for nuclear research. Beyond here a left turn leads to the **Church of Santa Caterina del Sasso** (➤ 151),

The Stresa to Monte Mottarone cable-car offers great views

At **Laveno**, the other terminus for the lake's car ferry, a cable-car rises to the forest-clad peak that dominates the town. This journey is not for the faint-hearted as the transport is an open 'bucket' in which two people stand – excellent for the view but hard going if you are afraid of heights. Back on the lakeside a twisting road leads to **Luino**, where an *Adoration of the Magi*, attributed to Bernardino Luini, can be seen in the Church of San Pietro.

TAKING A BREAK

On the western side of the lake, Stresa's **Piazza Cadorna** is the best place for a coffee, and excellent for people-watching. There is nothing as good on the eastern side, though there are good cafés near Laveno's port. For freshwater fish, the restaurants on Isola Pescatori serve it as fresh as anywhere in Italy.

✚ 196 B4
Castello Visconti
✉ Locarno ☎ 0041 91 7563461 🕐 Apr–Oct Tue–Sun 10–12, 2–5 🎫 Moderate

Villa Taranto
✉ Pallanza ☎ 0323 31533 🕐 Mar–Oct daily 9–7 🎫 Expensive

Isola Madre
☎ 0323 31261 🕐 Easter–Oct daily 9–5.30 🎫 Expensive

Villa Pallavicino
☎ 0323 32407 🕐 Mar–Nov daily 9–6 🎫 Expensive

LAGO DI MAGGIORE: INSIDE INFO

Top tip **Villa Taranto** is at its best in April, when 80,000 tulips bloom, and, a little later, when the azaleas and rhododendrons are in flower.

One to miss The huge **statue of San Carlo Borromeo** near Arona – 23.5m (77ft) tall and standing on a 12m (40ft) plinth – can be climbed (inside), but the statue is copper and in summer is oven-like.

3 Varese and its Lakes

Close to Lake Maggiore's southeastern shore there is a series of three small lakes and the city of Varese, a modern city grown prosperous on various light industries (particularly shoemaking), but with an interesting old centre.

The centre of the city has some beautiful 16th-century buildings

Varese

The city site was settled in pre-Roman times, but little of the town predates the 16th century. At its heart is the **Basilica di San Vittore**, built around 1600 to a design by Pellegrino Tibaldi (1527–96). The detached, 72m (235ft) Campanile del Bernascone is a local landmark named after its architect, Giuseppe Bernascone, a local man. Nearby, the **Baptistery of San Giovanni** is Varese's oldest building, dating from the 12th century. Inside there are what many believe to be the finest Lombard frescoes in the country – a series of Apostles, a Crucifixion, Madonna and Child – and an 8th-century font.

VARESE AND ITS LAKES: INSIDE INFO

Top tip If you are visiting **Arcuméggia** (➤ 152) try to arrive early, as parking is very difficult in the village.

From the old centre it is a short walk to the gardens of the **Palazzo Estense**, an 18th-century baroque mansion built as a summerhouse by Francesco II Este, Duke of Modena.

North of Varese is **Monte Campo dei Fiori**, on top of which sits the now neglected art nouveau Grand Hotel. From it steps led to three crosses and the 'Panoramic Balcony of Lombardy'. On a clear day the view includes Monte Rosa, the peaks of the Bernese Oberland, Varese and the local lakes.

Heading back down the mountain you reach a **Sacro Monte** with 14 frescoed chapels leading to the **Church of Santa Maria del Monte** and a small village of art nouveau houses. There are two museums here, one of the devotional art collection of Baron Baroffio, **Museo Baroffio**, the other with works of the sculptor Ludovico Pogliaghi (1857–1950).

South of Varese, in **Castiglione Olona**, there are two museums, the **Palazzo Branda Museo** and **Museo della Collegiata**.

Looking across the lake to the village of Oltrona

TAKING A BREAK

The cafés and restaurants of old Varese are the best, but if you are visiting Isolino Virginia try the little restaurant there, or take a picnic and enjoy the tranquillity.

✚ 196 C4
Museo Baroffio
✉ Sacro Monte ☎ 0332 212042 🕐 Apr–Oct Thu, Sat and Sun 9.30–12.30, 3–6.30 💶 Moderate

Palazzo Branda Museo
✉ Castiglione Olona ☎ 0331 858301 🕐 Apr–Sep Tue–Sat 9–12, 3–6, Sun 10.30–12.30, 3–6; Oct–Mar Sun 3–5 💶 Moderate

Museo della Collegiata
✉ Castiglione Olona ☎ 0331 858903 🕐 Apr–Sep Tue–Sun 9.30–12.30, 3–6; Oct–Mar Tue–Sun 10–12, 2.30–5.30 💶 Moderate

4 Lago di Lugano

Lake Lugano is shaped like a cartoon fox, nose at Ponte Tresa, ear at Agno, feet at Porto Ceresio and Capolago, and a huge tail all the way to Porlezza. Of the fox, all but his throat and chest, from Ponte Tresa to Porto Ceresio, and the tip of the tail are in Switzerland.

Lugano Town

Lugano is a marvellous city, beautifully set in a sheltered bay of the lake and framed by wooded peaks. Although a good resort town, and an excellent centre for exploration, Lugano is most famous for its art. In the **Church of Santa Maria degli Angioli**, at the southern end of the lakeside promenade (Riva Vela), there are frescoes by Bernardino Luini. Franciscan friars built the church and Luini completed his works while staying as their guest. The huge Passion is considered to be Luini's masterpiece. Some experts regard him to be equal of Leonardo, who had once been his teacher.

Closer to the centre of town, the **Museo Cantonale d'Arte** concentrates on 19th- and 20th- century art, and includes works by Klee and Renoir. The **Villa Favorita** was once the home of the Thyssen-Bornemisza art collection, one of the world's most famous private collections. The 'old masters' have now been rehoused in Madrid, Spain, leaving a collection of European and American modern art.

Mountains above the lake

From Lugano two funicular rides reach the top of the framing hills, **Monte Brè** to the east and **Monte San Salvatore** to the

Lugano offers excellent retail therapy

south. Each has a restaurant at the top (and a small village in the case of Monte Brè) and expansive views. Another fine view is that from the top of **Monte Generoso**, reached by a rack and pinion railway from Capolago at the southernmost tip of the lake. You will have to work a little harder to get the

best from it because the train doesn't make it to the top – you have to climb the last hundred or so feet.

Equally good, but much more difficult to reach, is the view from **Sighignola**. The panorama from this (Italian) viewpoint includes Monte Rosa, the Matterhorn, the Bernese Oberland and a stunning view of the lake. To reach it follow Lake Como's western shore northwards to Argegno, turning left there to pass through the villages of the Intelvi Valley. There is a café at the viewpoint: the massive ruins are the legacy of a failed attempt to link Campione to Italy by means of a cable-car.

The view to Monte Generoso from Arogno

The Swiss Lake
Below Sighignola is **Campione d'Italia** (► 152), the most

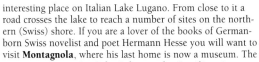

interesting place on Italian Lake Lugano. From close to it a road crosses the lake to reach a number of sites on the northern (Swiss) shore. If you are a lover of the books of German-born Swiss novelist and poet Hermann Hesse you will want to visit **Montagnola**, where his last home is now a museum. The writer is buried at nearby Gentilino. At Melide there is **Swissminiatur** (► 152), while at Morcote the **Scherrer Parco** has trees and statues overlooking the lake.

TAKING A BREAK

If it's not one of the cafés/restaurants on Lugano's lake promenade then it has to be one in Campione d'Italia.

✠ 196 C4

Museo Cantonale d'Arte
✉ Piazza Manzoni 7 (but entrance at Via Canova 10), Lugano ☎ 0041 91 9104780 ⏰ Wed–Sun 10–5, Tue 2–5 💷 Expensive

Monte Brè Funicular
✉ Lugano ☎ 0800 7228 ⏰ Apr–Oct daily 9–6.45 (9am–10pm in Jul and Aug) 💷 Moderate

Monte San Salvatore Funicular
✉ Lugano ☎ 0041 91 9852828 ⏰ Daily 10–6 💷 Moderate

Monte Generoso Ferrovia
✉ Capolago ☎ 0419 6481105 ⏰ Mar–Nov daily 10–4.45 💷 Expensive

Museo Hermann Hesse
✉ Montagnola ☎ 0041 91 9933770 ⏰ Mar–Oct Tue–Sun 10–6.30; Nov–Feb Sat–Sun 10–5.30 💷 Moderate

Scherrer Parco
✉ Morcote ☎ 0041 91 9962125 ⏰ Mar–Oct daily 10–5 (10–6 in Jul and Aug) 💷 Moderate

---

LAGO DI LUGANO: INSIDE INFO

Top tip Hire a pedalo at Lugano and enjoy a terrific view of the city, Monte Brè and Monte San Salvatore from the lake.

Hidden gems At Gandria the **Museo Dogane Svizzero** (tel 0041 91 9104811, open daily 1.30–5.30, moderate) is a museum of smuggling, with exhibits on the surprising and often hilarious dodges used to transfer goods from Italy to Switzerland.
• From Porlezza a winding road heads north to the **Val Cavergna**, a valley of unspoilt beauty and charming villages.

⑤ Lago di Como

The inverted Y of Lake Como has an odd feature – there is only one outflowing river, the Adda, leaving the eastern lake arm (often called Lake Lecco) at Lecco. As a consequence, heavy rain that floods the northern lake and its western arm can cause an increase in water level. If it rains hard enough – and several times a year it does – Piazza Cavour, Como town's lakeside square, becomes part of the lake.

Como town

Despite the flooding risk, the Como city site has a long history, having been settled during the Bronze Age. The Romans took it from the Gauls, Julius Caesar himself rebuilding it and persuading 5,000 settlers to populate it. Piazza Cavour, with its steamer quays, is the main square. From it the prominent circular Tempio Voltiano, home of the museum to Alessandro Volta (► 23), can be seen.

From the square, take Via Plinio on its left edge (as viewed from the lake), soon reaching **Piazza Duomo**. The city's cathedral is a remarkable building. It took 400 years to complete, which is why the façade on Piazza Duomo is Gothic, while the eastern end in Piazza Verdi is Renaissance, though the dome itself was not added until the 18th century. The niche statues of the western façade are of the Elder and Younger Plinys. The façade is attached to the early 13th-

The Basilica di San Fedele is a medieval masterpiece

century Broletto (the medieval town hall), built in Romanesque style, one of few secular survivals of the form in northern Italy. The adjacent **Torre del Commune** became a clock tower when the upper storey was added 200 years later. The splendour of these buildings in Piazza Duomo is a tribute to Como's medieval prosperity, which was largely based on silk, an industry still prominent in the city. There is a silk museum, **Museo Didattico della Seta**, in Via Castelnuovo and **La Tessitura**, in Viale Roosevelt, makes and sells silk products.

Across the railway line of the Ferrovia Nord, a private railway between Como and Stazione Nord, Milan, is the **Casa del Fascio** (➤ 20) in Piazza del Popolo.

Behind Piazza Cavour there is a grid of old streets, some still lined with houses, many of which are now shops. At the heart of this area is **Piazza San Fedele**, the old corn market and the most picturesque part of the town. The square is named after the church (entrance in Via Vittorio Emanuele II, on

the other side from the square), a 12th-century masterpiece by the Maestri Comacini, a tightly knit group of architects and stone-masons whose fame spread across Europe.

Continuing through the old town you will reach Porta Vittoria, an ancient towered gateway. Church lovers will also want to visit the **Basilica of San Abbondio**, a superb Romanesque building, while those with a more macabre taste might head for the **Baradello Tower**. Built in 1158, it rises above the city's southwestern edge. Legend has it that after Napa Torriani, a local lord, was defeated by Milan's Viscontis, he and his family were placed in cages hanging outside the tower. Half-starved and exposed to the elements, his family died one by one and in despair he smashed his head on the tower wall.

Traditional and tempting methods of drying fish are still practised in Sala Comacina

The Western Lake

From Como town follow the road for Cernobbio, passing the fine 17th-century Villa Olmo on the southwestern edge of Como, beside the lake. At Cernobbio the park around Villa Erba is a peaceful place, while on the other side of the town **Villa d'Este**, built in the 16th century, is now Lake Como's most exclusive hotel. It has beautiful gardens, which cross the lakeside road via a bridge, and a swimming pool floating on the lake. North again, at Argegno, a cable-car rises to Pigra for a panoramic view of the lake. Beyond Argegno the campanile at Ospedaletto, which has a Romanesque base and Gothic turret, is one of the most photographed buildings on the lake. Offshore lies Isola Comacina (➤ 10).

Ahead, Balbianello Point pokes out into the lake. At its lake end is **Villa del Balbianello** (➤ 153). When the road regains the lake the Azalean Riviera begins, a particularly fertile strip, with citrus and olive trees and the gardens of **Villa Carlotta** (➤ 153), Lake Como's most famous villa.

Menággio, at the northern edge of the Azalean Riviera, was an important trading centre, an easy route linking it to Lake Lugano and Switzerland. Car ferries shuttle between here, Bellágio and Varenna. Menággio also has fine villas and its equitable winter climate was a favourite with British politician Winston Churchill and Venice's Cardinal Roncalli (before he became Pope John XXIII). North of Menággio there are several charming villages, including Dongo, where Mussolini was arrested in 1945.

The harbour and waterfront at Menággio on Lake Como

The Eastern Lake
The lake road rounds Como's northern end (through the Piano di Spagna), before heading south to Varenna and **Villa Monastero** – the finest villa on the eastern shore. Built in 1208 for Cistercian nuns, it became a private villa in 1569 and is now a research centre for hydrobiology and lake geomorphology, but the gardens are open to the public.

From Varenna a new road will hurry you to Lecco, below the hills of the **Grigna** (➤ 154). Lecco was the birthplace of Manzoni (➤ 24) and there is a statue of him in Piazza Manzoni and a museum to him in the villa where he spent his early life, **Villa Manzoni**. Another fine building, Palazzo Beljioioso, houses the **Lecco Town Museum**.

The Central Lake
The Como and Lecco arms of the lake were created when a triangular mass of hard rock split the glacier that carved the

now water-filled valleys. Today the triangular mass splits the wind, and the headland is known as La Punta Spartivento, 'the point that divides the wind'. Behind the point lies **Bellágio** (➤ 154), Lake Como's most romantic town.

TAKING A BREAK

The pavement cafés of Como's Piazza Duomo and Piazza San Fedele are excellent, but there are possibilities in all the lake's towns and larger villages.

✚ 197 D4
Museo Didattico della Seta
✉ Via Castelnuovo 1, Como ☎ 031 303180; www.museosetacomo.it
🕐 Tue–Fri 9–12, 3–6 💰 Expensive

La Tessitura
✉ Viale Roosevelt 2, Como ☎ 031 321666 🕐 Daily 10–8 💰 Free

Villa Monastero
✉ Varenna ☎ 0341 295450 🕐 Gardens: Mar–Nov daily 9–7.
Villa: Mar–Nov Sat 1–5, Sun 10–1, 2–6 💰 Moderate

Villa Manzoni
✉ Via Guanella 7, Lecco ☎ 0341 481247 🕐 Tue–Sun, 9.30–5.30
💰 Moderate

Pavement cafés are central to the Italian lifestyle

Lecco Town Museum
✉ Palazzo Beljioioso, Corso Matteotti 32, Lecco ☎ 0341 481248
🕐 Tue–Sun 9.30–2 💰 Free

LAGO DI COMO: INSIDE INFO

Top tip Parking in Como town is a nightmare. Arrive early and park in Piazza Volta (fee) or use the multi-storey near Porta Vittorio and walk into town.

Hidden gem Abbazia di Piona (tel 0341 940331, open daily 9.30–12, 2–5, free), on the northeastern shore near Colico, is easy to miss. Built by the Cluniac order, this beautiful 12th-century building is now home to Cistercian monks. There is also a shop selling the monks' herbal liqueur and other gifts.

At Your Leisure

6 Isola San Giúlio

Having crossed Lake Orta on his cloak (▶ 134), San Giúlio built the first church on the island; according to legend, he used wolves to pull his cart as they were quicker than oxen. The present church, dedicated to the saint, dates from the late 9th century. It was built on the site of Giúlio's original but has been restored at various times. Inside there are excellent medieval frescoes, but the greatest treasure is the *ambo* (pulpit) in black Oira marble, which dates from the 11th or 12th century. On the pulpit San Giúlio is shown in relief: he leans on his sword, apparently exhausted from the effort of chasing away dragons. The church used to display 'dragon' bones too, but these are presently out of sight, perhaps because the general consensus that they were from humans could not be ignored. However, the remains of San Giúlio are still visible.

The church and convent take up almost all of the island, but a circular walk through narrow alleys reveals some interesting houses, views of the lakes and a couple of good cafés.

➕ 196 A4

7 Isola Bella

It is a matter of opinion whether the palazzo and gardens of Isola Bella, off Stresa, are a flamboyant masterpiece or an orgy of conspicuous bad taste. Whatever your view, the complex should not be ignored. When Count Carlo III Borromeo first saw the island it was flat and rocky. What he wanted was the appearance of a ship anchored off-shore, so he created a terraced garden 40m (131ft) high with a slope from the southern tip: look hard and suspend judgement and it does look a little ship-like. The count named his island after his wife, though Isola Isabella was soon shortened to the present form.

The gardens are Italianate, enhanced by white peacocks but with an over-abundance of very poor quality, reproduction sculpture. The baroque palazzo has the same mix of the sublime and the less so. The chandeliers of Murano glass, the great hall with its pale blue walls, the

Carefully constructed focal points are a feature of the gardens of Isola Bella

art and the Flemish tapestries are quite superb (as are many of the other rooms), but then there are the grottoes. These are six mosaic-lined caves full of curiosities.

A magical item that should not be missed is the **Puppet Theatre**. It has the most extraordinary characters – a giant that turns into elves, a sedan

---

chair turning into a woman. And all the puppets are exquisitely carved.

🞢 196 B4 ✉ Stresa, Lake Maggiore ☎ 0323 30556 🕐 Mid-Mar to Oct daily 9–5.30 💰 Expensive

8 Rocca di Angera

The steep road to the castle from the town passes the Cava del Lupo, the wolves' den, occupied in prehistoric times and later the site of a Roman temple. The castle itself, which dominates southern Lake Maggiore, also has Roman origins, though the basis of what now stands is 11th century. It was modified and extended by the Viscontis and Borromeos until the 15th century.

The castle's rooms are now bare, which gives them a strange, brooding feel. In the Sala di Ceremonie (Ceremony Room) there are detached frescoes from the Borromeo palazzo in Milan, while the splendid Sala di Giustizia (Justice Room) has frescoes of Visconti battles. The views from the battlements are

Magnificent frescoes decorate the vaulted ceilings of the Sala di Giustizia

inspiring, and the castle is now home to the **Museo della Bambola** (Doll Museum) with a collection of 19th- and 20th-century dolls, including many from the renowned Turin doll-making Lenci company.

🞢 196 B4 ✉ Lake Maggiore ☎ 0331 931300 🕐 Mar–Nov Mon–Sat 9.30–5.30, Sun 9–6

Museo della Bambola
✉ Rocca di Angera 🕐 Mar–Nov Mon–Sat 9.30–5.30, Sun 9–6
💰 Expensive (joint ticket)

9 Santa Caterina del Sasso

In the 13th century Alberto Bessozi, a local smuggler and userer, was sailing on Lake Maggiore when a sudden storm threatened to sink the boat and drown him. Alberto promised God that if his life was spared he would dedicate his life to prayer. Miraculously he was thrown onto a ledge below steep cliffs. There he spent the last 40 years of his life sustained by food lowered in a bucket by local folk, and drinking spring water. When plague threatened the area Alberto's prayers were

Santa Caterina del Sasso clings to a rocky outcrop overhanging the lakeside

houses have been used as canvasses by contemporary Italian artists and there are now more than 150 works to discover. Not great art, but certainly enormous fun.

🔤 196 B4

🆔 Swissminiatur

Situated close to Melide, near Lake Lugano's northern shore, the Swissminiatur is a 1:25 scale park of the best of Switzerland. Spread over a 1ha (2.5-acre) site are re-creations of the main sights of all the Swiss cantons – mountains, buildings, etc. The cable-cars and boats all work and a 3km (2-mile) model railway threads its way through the site.

🔤 196 C4 ✉ Melide, Lake Lugano ☎ 0041 91 6401060 🕐 Mid-Mar to Oct Daily 9–6 💷 Expensive

🆔 Campione d'Italia

In the 8th century a local lord gave, in perpetuity, the land which is now

The small fresco above this water fountain in Arcuméggia is by Enzo Morell

said to have saved the locals. A church was built on his ledge and later, in the 14th century, a small monastery was erected beside it. Both were spared destruction when falling boulders wedged themselves into a crevice above Alberto's tomb. Today, Santa Caterina is a joy, steep steps leading to the church, which houses Alberto's mummified rather than decayed body – yet another miracle.

🔤 196 B4 ✉ Lake Maggiore ☎ 0332 647172 🕐 Apr–Oct daily 8.30–12, 2.30–6; Nov–Feb Sat–Sun 9–12, 2–5; Mar daily 9–12, 2–5 💷 Free ❓ For those wishing to avoid the steep climb down (and back) from the clifftop car park, the church can be reached by lake steamers from Stresa

🆔 Arcuméggia

Set high above the Valcuvia, near Varese, the ancient village of Arcuméggia is something of an outdoor art exhibition. Since the 1950s the external walls of the

Campione d'Italia to the Church of Sant'Ambrogio in Milan. Amazingly, when the Swiss over-ran Milanese holdings near Lake Lugano they honoured the gift. Despite being completely surrounded by Switzerland, using the Swiss postal service and Swiss currency, the area remains resolutely Italian. In medieval times the local builders, the Maestri Campionesi, were renowned for their architectural skills: they built the Church of San Pietro which, together with the Madonna dei Ghirli and its frescoes, are the highlights of the town. There is also a casino, which provides much of the town's prosperity; the Swiss cross the lake in numbers to take advantage of the gaming and cabarets.

➕ 196 C4

🔢 Villa del Balbianello

On Saturday and Sunday the villa occupying the small headland that protrudes from Lake Como's Azalean Riviera can be reached on foot from Lenno. Ignore this option, favouring a weekday visit when you must travel by boat, arriving at the most romantic quay in northern Italy, a statued breakwater with a stone staircase leading to a verdant garden. Built as the palazzo of the Balbiati family, the villa was later a rest home for Franciscan monks and then remodelled by Cardinal Angelo Divini. It houses the mountaineering collection of Guido Monzino, leader of the first successful Italian Everest expedition in 1973, and one-time owner, but is rarely open to the public. However, the gardens and views more than compensate.

➕ 197 D4 ✉ Lenno, Lake Como
☎ 0344 56110 🕐 Gardens only:
Mar–Oct Thu–Tue 10–6 💶 Moderate

🔢 Villa Carlotta

The most famous of all Lake Como's villas stands across the water from Bellágio. Most visitors assume the 'C' at the entrance is for Carlotta, but it isn't. It stands for Clerici, the family who built the villa in the 18th century. The name derives from the daughter of a later owner. The Sommariva family bought the villa in the 19th century and it took its present form under their direction. Inside there are many art treasures, the most important being works by Canova (including *Cupid and Psyche* and *Mary Magdalene*, wonderful portrayals of love and despair) and a remarkable frieze by the Icelander Bertel Thorvaldsen. The villa is a gem, but the gardens are even better. In April and May, when the azaleas, camellias and rhododendrons are in bloom, there is no better place on the lakes.

➕ 197 D4 ✉ Tremezzo, Lake Como
☎ 0344 40405 🕐 Apr–Sep daily 9–6;
Mar and Oct 9–5 💶 Expensive
❓ No photography in the villa

Antonio Canova's
Cupid and Psyche
was completed
in 1824

15 Bellágio

Often referred to as the 'Pearl of the Lake' and occasionally claimed to be the most beautiful town in Europe, Bellágio is the most visited place on Lake Como. The lake front is a montage of elegant buildings from which steep, stepped alleys lead up to the Romanesque Church of San Giacomo. At the northern end of the town the Grand Hotel Villa Serbelloni takes its name from the villa behind it, now a study centre, though the surrounding parkland is open for guided tours. At the other end of town **Villa Melzi d'Eryl** is the

Villa Melzi d'Eryl
✉ Bellágio, Lake Como ☎ 031 950318 ⏱ Mar–Oct daily 9–6
💰 Expensive

16 Grigna Mountains

To the north of Lecco lies the Grigna, a displaced part of the Dolomites, lifted up and placed here beside Lake Como. The Grigna is a land of rock towers and arêtes, rising to the 2,410m (7,881) high point of Grigna Settontrionale, a name usually shortened to Grignone (Big Grigna). The peak lies at the north end of the range: to the south is Grigna

The picturesque waterfront at Bellágio, Lake Como

finest neo-classical building on any lake. The Hungarian composer Franz Liszt stayed here in 1837: his daughter Cosima was born in Como.

The parkland surrounding the villa is the equal of that at Villa Serbelloni, particularly when the azaleas are in bloom. The views from here – as they are from every part of town – are outstanding.

➕ 197 D4
Villa Serbelloni
✉ Bellagio, Lake Como ☎ 031 951555 ⏱ Parkland: guided tours only Apr–Oct Tue–Sun 11am and 3.30pm
💰 Expensive

Meridionale, 2,184m,(7,142ft), which is known, of course, as Grignetta (Little Grigna).

This is splendid walking country, the best route to the Grignone passing through a rock arch and needing fixed chains to reach the summit cross and the *rifugio*, where welcome refreshments are sold. From the summit, on a clear day, both the Matterhorn in Switzerland and Florence are visible.

For a more relaxed walk, take the cable-car from northeast Lecco to the Piano d'Erna. It rises past sheer cliffs (up which a *Via Ferrata* climbs, ► 13) to reach an area of flat pasture with a café and expansive views.
➕ 197 D4

Where to... Stay

Prices
Expect to pay per double room, per night
€ under €70   €€ €70–€130   €€€ over €130

LAGO D'ORTA

L'Approdo €€€
A modern, family-friendly hotel with a big garden beside the lake, a heated, outdoor swimming pool and tennis courts. Boats for hire.

✚ 196 A4 ⌂ Corso Roma 80, 28028
Pettenasco ☎ 0323 89345;
www.lagodortahotels.com
Ⓒ Closed early Jan–late Feb

Belvedere €
This is arguably the best hotel on the lake, with an attractive garden and a solarium.

✚ 196 A4 ⌂ Via Belvedere 8, 28896
Quarna Sopra ☎ Tel/fax: 0323 826198

LAGO DI COMO

Albergo Firenze €€
Just a two-minute walk away from the lake, the Firenze has a cosmopolitan feel. The multilingual staff are very friendly and helpful, and most of the rooms have parquet floors, lake views and modern décor. Breakfast is served buffet style, with bowls of buns and spreads to complement the plates of cheese and ham. The hotel is within walking distance of the harbour for trips on the lake.

✚ 196 C4 ⌂ Piazza Volta 16, 22100
Como ☎ 031 300 333;
www.albergofirenze.it

Barchetta Excelsior €€€
Overlooking Piazza Cavour, the city's main square. Comfortable rooms with modern décor and a restaurant. Secure parking available nearby.

✚ 196 C4 ⌂ Piazza Cavour 1,
22100 Como ☎ 031 302622;
www.hotelbarchetta.com

Central €€
Set in the centre of the town just a short walk from the lake steamer quay. Small, but recently refurbished to a good standard. Very friendly and comfortable.

✚ 196 C4 ⌂ Via Regina 39, 22012
Cernobbio ☎ 031 511411;
www.albergo-centrale.com

Grand Hotel Tremezzo €€€
Magnificent building close to Villa Carlotta. Some rooms have balconies overlooking the lake. Exceptional gardens with a panoramic view of the lake.

✚ 197 D4 ⌂ Via Regina 8, 22019
Tremezzo ☎ 0344 42491;
www.grandhoteltremezzo.com
Ⓒ Closed mid-Nov to Mar

Moderno €
The Lecco arm of the lake tends to be overlooked, but if you are wanting to explore the area, or to enjoy the Grigna mountains, then the city is a good base. The outside looks a bit uninviting, but take heart, the rooms are comfortable and well appointed and the staff are friendly. It does not have a restaurant, which means you have to go out for breakfast – but there is a lot of local choice.

✚ 197 D4 ⌂ Piazza Diaz 5, 22053
Lecco ☎ 0341 286519; email:
hotel.moderno@promo.it

Villa d'Este €€€
A super-luxury hotel with every conceivable facility. The villa was built in 1557 and has been a hotel since 1873. Superb art, furnishings and a glorious garden, plus a floating swimming pool. Garage parking is available.

LAGO DI LUGANO

Hotel Campione €€

Despite the name, the hotel is just outside the entrance arch to Campione and therefore in Switzerland. Recently renovated and very comfortable. Good for children as there is a separate pool for them away from the adult pool. There is a terrace overlooking the lake. The restaurant on the terrace is excellent.

🞧 196 C4 ⊠ Via Campione 62, CH22060 Campione d'Italia ☎ 0041 91 6401616; www.hotel-campione.ch

Hotel due Lac €

Well sited beside the lake and a short distance from the border town of Ponte Tresa. Simply but comfortably furnished, and the restaurant is excellent.

🞧 196 C4 ⊠ Viale Ungheria 19,

21037 Lavena Ponte Tresa ☎ 0332 550308; www.dulac.bbk.org

LAGO DI MAGGIORE

Camin Hotel Luino €€€

Lovely 19th-century building across the road from the lake and a short walk of the town centre. Large, frescoed rooms. Booking essential.

🞧 196 B4 ⊠ Viale Dante 35, 21016 Luino ☎ 0332 530118; www. caminhotelluino.com ⊘ Closed for a week at Christmas and Jan

Dei Tigli €

This is a simple, but very clean and neat, and very friendly hotel, set on the lake. There is no restaurant, but only a short walk from several possibilities.

🞧 196 B4 ⊠ Via Paletta 20, 21021 Angera ☎ 0331 930836; www.hoteldeitigli.com

La Fontana €€

This elegant villa is in beautiful gardens a little way out of town so

it is really only suitable if you have a car. The rooms are spacious and well appointed and the staff friendly. There is no restaurant, but Stresa is only a short drive away and there is one across the road.

🞧 196 B4 ⊠ Strada statale del Sempione 1, 28838 Stresa ☎ 0323 32707; www.lafontanahotel.com ⊘ Closed Dec and Jan

Grand Hotel des Iles Borromées €€€

The grandest hotel on the lake, with a helicopter pad and an on-site doctor. The building, luxuriously furnished, dates from 1861. Garage parking.

🞧 196 B4 ⊠ Corso Umberto I 67, 28838 Stresa ☎ 0323 938938; www.borromees.it

Verbano €€€

Once the day visitors have gone home you will have the island to yourself. The hotel has lovely views of the lake and is very well decorated. Reasonable restaurant.

🞧 196 B4 ⊠ Via Ugo Ara 12, 28838 Isola Pescatori ☎ 0323 30408; www.hotelverbano.it ⊘ Closed early Jan–late Feb

VARESE

Bologna €€

An 18th-century monastery has been restored to make this comfortable hotel in the centre of the old city. It has a restaurant and the owners are proud of their home cooking.

🞧 196 C4 ⊠ Via Broggi 7, 21100 Varese ☎ 0332 232100; www.albergobologna.it ⊘ Closed for 2 weeks in Feb and Aug

City €€

This has the advantages of a city hotel, but also easy access to the western lakes. Close to the railway station. No restaurant, but many within walking distance. Garage.

🞧 196 C4 ⊠ Via Medaglie d'Oro 35, 21100 Varese ☎ 0332 281304; www.cityhotelvarese.com

Where to...
Eat and Drink

Prices
Expect to pay for a three-course meal for one, excluding drinks and service
€ under €30   €€ €30–€60   €€€ over €60

LAGO D'ORTA

Trattoria Toscana €
Surprisingly inexpensive for one of the best restaurants on the lake, with a long and inventive menu. Lake fish is one speciality, but there are others – try the 'mountain recipe' gnocchi.

➕ 196 A4 ✉ Via Mazzini 153, 28026 Omegna ☎ 0323 62460 🕓 Closed Wed

Villa Crespi €€€
A 19th-century villa set in parkland and considered the best eating place on the lake by local gourmets.

chose your meal live from a tank. Booking is essential.

➕ 197 D4 ✉ Via Valsecchi 5/7, 23900 Lecco ☎ 0341 498103 🕓 Dinner only. Closed Mon and Tue, also 1–10 Jan and Aug

Barchetta €
This restaurant is tucked out of sight in the heart of the town. Search it out for a simple menu, but excellent cooking and very friendly service.

➕ 196 C4 ✉ Piazza Roma 2, 22010 Argegno ☎ 031 821105 🕓 Closed Mon

LAGO DI COMO

Al Porticciolo €€
Al Porticciolo, considered to be the best restaurant in town is particularly famous for its fish – you can

There is a touch of the orient about the cooking, though many of the recipes are based on traditional themes. There are a few rooms too, if you wish to stay overnight.

➕ 196 A4 ✉ Via Fava 18, 28016 Orta San Giulio (the villa is actually 2km/1 mile east of the town) ☎ 0322 911902 🕓 Closed Wed lunch, Mon and Jan–Mar

Bilacus €€
Bilacus is one of the best places to eat in this fairytale village. The rooftop terrace (not much of a view except into the steep street below, but as romantic as could be imagined as the sun sets) is superb, as is the food. The fish and saffron/mushroom risotto are famous. No praise too high. Booking in advance is advised.

Inexpensive, and one of the best places in town – just watch the queues form in the early evening. Excellent cooking with arguably the best *spaghetti al pomodoro* on the lake.

Le Colonne €

➕ 196 C4 ✉ Piazza Mazzini, 22100 Como ☎ 031 2661666 🕓 Closed Tue Nov–Feb

Imperialino €€€
Now the main lake road has bypassed Moltrasio, peace and quiet are added to the marvellous lake views in this small, elegant restaurant. It is very friendly, and offers a very high-quality menu and cooking. Local dishes are a speciality, but the menu is not limited.

➕ 196 C4 ✉ Via Antica Regina 26, 22010 Moltrasio ☎ 031 346600 🕓 Closed Mon

➕ 197 D4 ✉ Via Serbelloni 32, 22021 Bellagio ☎ 031 950480 🕓 Closed Mon and Nov–Mar

LAGO DI LUGANO

Da Candida €€

A simply wonderful restaurant. A lovely old building, excellent service and a menu that is a combination of the simple and the exciting. Try the lamb dishes, or something a little more exotic.

➕ 196 C4 ⊠ Via Marco 4, 22060 Campione d'Italia
☎ 0041 91 6497541 Ⓒ Closed Mon, Tue lunch and 3 weeks in Jul

LAGO DI MAGGIORE

Lo Scalo €€€

One of the best restaurants on the northwestern shore, with a picturesque terrace overlooking the lake. The menu changes frequently but the chef usually has one or two interesting rabbit dishes plus traditional Piemontian dishes.

➕ 196 B5 ⊠ Piazza Vittorio Emanuele 32, 28822 Cannóbio
☎ 0323 71480 Ⓒ Closed Mon, Tue lunch, Jan, Feb and Nov

Piemontese €€

As the name implies, the food here is typical of Piedmonte, with a large range of cheeses on offer. You'll find the restaurant tucked away in the centre of the old town and you can eat under a pergola.

➕ 196 B4 ⊠ Via Mazzini 25, 33040 Stresa
☎ 0323 30235 Ⓒ Closed Mon, Dec and Jan

Trattoria Campania €€

This is an extremely attractive trattoria serving traditional dishes made with local produce. The staff here are very friendly, helping to create a good atmosphere, and they are also very helpful, particularly with suggestions of what is in season.

➕ 196 B4 ⊠ Via Vergante 1, 28041 Arona ☎ 0322 57294
Ⓒ Closed Tue and 2 weeks in Nov. Mon dinner only last week Jun–first week Jul

La Vecchia Angera €€

Along with the extremely pleasant atmosphere here, you'll find a simple, but interesting menu. The tourist menu is exceptional value, but despite this the clientele is mostly local and the atmosphere is delightfully Italian.

➕ 196 B4 ⊠ Via Borromeo 10, 21021 Angera
☎ 0331 930224 Ⓒ Closed Mon

Unione €€

It could be argued that the only authentic place to eat lake fish is on Isola Pescatori, and it is likely that the basis of your chosen dish was landed last night. It will have been cooked to perfection – in an unfussy style – and in a setting that couldn't be more delightful or romantic. Free ferry in the evenings from/to Stresa.

➕ 196 B4 ⊠ Via Lungola 16, Isola Pescatori, 28049 Stresa
☎ 0323 933798
Ⓒ Closed Thu in Oct and Nov–Mar

VARESE

Al Vecchio Convento €€€

Arguably the best place in town – you need to book in advance to be sure of a table in the main room with its large fireplace. The specialities include risottos and Tuscan dishes. There is a large wine list and the menu is changed seasonally.

➕ 196 C4 ⊠ Viale Borri 348, 17019 Varese ☎ 0332 261005
Ⓒ Closed Sun dinner, Mon and last 2 weeks in Aug

La Bussola €

Very elegant and with something to suit all tastes. It is both a traditional restaurant and a pizzeria. Good cooking and excellent service. The terrace area is very picturesque and there is also a banquet room.

➕ 196 C4 ⊠ Via Marconi 28, 21033 Cittiglio ☎ 0332 60229;
www.hotellabussola.it
Ⓒ Closed Tue

Where to... Shop

The best places to shop are the larger towns, particularly Varese and, to a lesser extent, Como, and also Lugano if you venture into Switzerland. The towns and villages along the lakes cater for tourists, and so have lots of souvenirs and the odd art gallery.

ANTIQUES

There are two good outlets in Cernobbio on Lake Como, **Aurelio Dotti** (11 Via Trento) and **Trouvailles** (34 Via Regina). In Como itself there are several interesting places near Piazza San Fedele, and **Antique Runner** (23 Via Rezzonico) is also worth exploring. If you are looking for

antique jewellery, head for **Galleria Bertola** (2 Contrada dei Monti) in Orta San Giulio.

ART GALLERIES

Galleries come and go around the lakes area, but more established outlets include **Borgovico 33** (33 Via Borgovico) in Como. **Pietrantonio** (5 Via Caminichetta) in Varese and **Zanella Arch Giulio** (15 Via Venegoni) in Gallarate are also long-standing outlets.

For something different, **Penelope** (26 Piazza Motta) in Orta San Giulio has prints on woven linen and hemp.

JEWELLERY

There are excellent gold- and silver-smiths in Italy, some of them working out of their own studios. More established outlets include several in Varese's Corso Matteotti, for instance **Auroom** at No 40 and Rigamonti at No 18. **Arte Orafa** in

Bellagio is the outlet for Giuseppe Steliano's original jewellery.

EMBROIDERY

Exquisite hand-embroidered table linen, underclothes and children's clothes are to be found at **Maddalena Ciapessoni** (Lungoloargo Mazzani) in Bellagio.

LEATHER

Every town and most villages have shops selling shoes and handbags, or coats and jackets.

SILK

Como is famous for its silk and has several shops, though mostly they sell only ties for men and scarves for women. **Inseta** (Piazza Cavour) has a wide range, as do **Frey** (36 Via Boldoni and 10 Via Garibaldi) and **Picci** (54 Via Vittorio Emanuele). In Bellagio, **Pierangelo Masciardi** is a modern silk

master using patterns based on Renaissance masterpieces. His shop is Arte e Moda (19 Salita Mella).

FACTORY OUTLETS

At Vertemate, close to the Fino Mornasco exit from the A8, south of Como, **Armani** has a factory. The silk-makers **Ratti** are close to the Lomazzo exit of the A9, while **Rossetti** has a factory between the Parabiago-Kegnano and Castellanza exits of the A8.

MARKETS

There are good general markets at **Domódossola** on Saturday; **Cannóbio** on Sunday; **Luino** on Wednesday; **Como** on Wednesday and Thursday mornings and all day Saturday; and **Lugano** on Tuesday and Friday mornings and all day Saturday. **Varenna** has an antiques market every third Sunday in the summer and **Lecco** one on Wednesday and Saturday.

Where to...
Be Entertained

SPORT AND LEISURE

Watersports

Sailing and windsurfing schools can be found at virtually every town and village on the lakes.

The lake water is not as warm as might be assumed – those inflowing rivers are coming from the Alps after all – but the calm conditions do give diving schools an advantage. There are good schools at Verbania on Lake Maggiore (**Subverbania**, tel: 0323 501305 and **Squadro Nautica**, tel: 0323 519100), at Caslano on Lake Lugano (**Lugano Sub Paradiso**, tel: 0041 91 9945777) and at Mandello Lario on the Lecco arm of Lake Como (**Mutevole**, tel: 0341 700769).

There are fewer waterskiing centres than might be imagined because fast motorboats do not mix well with sailing and other, quieter forms of activity. There is also a strong movement aimed at preserving the peace of the lakes. There are possibilities, however, at Omegna (**Sci Nautico Cusio**, tel: 0323 61365 and **Sci Nautico Omegna**, tel: 0323 868611), Stresa (**Club Nautico Stresa**, tel: 0323 30551), Cernobbio (**Centro Sci Nautico**, tel: 031 342232) and Lugano (**Club Nautico Lugano**, tel: 0041 91 9235733).

Adventure Sports

Walking is available on the high ridges and is particularly good on the Grigna mountains above Lecco.

The *Via Ferrata* (▶ 13) on the Resegone is the best in the area, but there are others, for instance on Monte Grona above Menàggio. Rock climbers will be entranced by a recent venture at Maccagno, on the northeastern shore of Lake Maggiore, where the techniques of indoor climbing walls have been added to a bridge and a section of natural cliff to create a fully protected outdoor climbing wall.

Mountain bikes and road cycles are now available for hire at many places on the lakes. At Guello, **Bellàgio Cavalcalario** (tel: 031 964814) offers downhill mountain bike trips.

There are paragliding schools that fly beginners at Lugano (**Alpe Foppa Monte Tamaro**, tel: 0041 91 9462303), Laveno (**Icaroo 2000**, tel: 0332 626212 – they fly from Sasso del Ferro at the top of the bucket ride) and at Guello, above Bellàgio (**Cavalcalario**, tel: 031 964814).

A less adventurous way of getting an aerial view is to take a hot-air balloon trip with **Balloon Team Lugano** (tel: 0041 91 9210672).

In winter there is skiing at Pian di Bobbio and Pian d'Erna above Lecco, and also on Monte Tamara, between lakes Maggiore and Lugano.

Golf

Golfing facilities are numerous, with courses at Stresa, Ascona, Lugano, Carimate (near the Lomazzo exit of the A8 south of Como), Travedonna Monate (west of Varese) and Lanzo d'Intelvi.

NIGHTLIFE

There are cinemas and discos in most large towns. Venues presently in vogue include:
Kelly Green (33 Via Lungolago Gramsci) in Omegna; **Desperados** (Via Al Forte 4) in Lugano; **Griffe** (12 Via Dandolo) in Varese; and **CFC** (Via S Abbondio) in Como.

Excursions

Excursions

There are a number of towns and cities within easy reach of the lakes region that are well worth a visit. Among these are Cremona and Mantova, to the south of Bréscia, and Vicenza, to the east of Verona. Each very different in character, they can all be reached comfortably in a day.

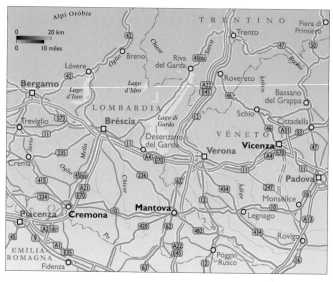

Cremona

As home of the modern violin and the world's most famous violin-maker, Cremona will be high on the itinerary of every lover of the instrument. But even if your interest in violins is only a passing one, you will find much to appreciate in the Renaissance heart of the city.

The Piazza del Comune can be very crowded when there is a festival

Torrazzo

If you had intended to do nothing else in Cremona than search out violins and violin-makers, and sample *torrone* (that illustrious mix of almonds, honey and egg white that some still call nougat, a sin akin to comparing grape juice with fine wine), you should add a third item to your list – a visit to **Piazza del Comune**. Here stands the **Torrazzo**, at 113m (370ft) the tallest campanile in Italy (and one of the tallest medieval towers in Europe). Begun in 1250, it was completed almost 50 years later when the Gothic lantern was added. In exchange for the climb up the 500-odd steps there is a fine view of the city.

Duomo and Stradivarius

The Torrazzo is linked by the Bertazzola, a double loggia, to the 12th-century **Duomo,** one of the best and most flamboyant Lombard Romanesque churches in Italy. The scrolling suggests the form found on the city's famous violins. Inside there are works by Pordenone and Romanino.

In the same piazza as the Duomo are the octagonal **Battistero di San Giovanni**, from the same period as the cathedral but less flamboyant; the **Loggia dei Militi**, dating from 1292 and once the meeting point of Cremona's citizen militia; and the **Palazzo del Comune**, built in the early 13th century for the city governors and still the town hall. The palazzo's Saletta dei Violini (Room of Violins) houses some of Cremona's most famous violins, including Stradivarius' Cremonese, made in 1715. There are other instruments by Andrea Amati and Giuseppe Guarneri. North of Piazza del Comune is Stradivarius' red marble **tombstone**.

Next, head north into Piazza Roma, bearing right to follow Via Manzoni. After 3,000m (3,270 yards) turn left along Via Ugolani Dati to reach the 16th-century Palazzo Affaitati, which houses the **Museo Civico** comprising a museum covering archaeology, the Stradivarius museum and an art gallery.

San Sigismondo

Cremona has many fine churches, particularly in the area between the Museo Civico and Palazzo del Comune, but to see the best take a 20-minute walk east of the palazzo or a ride on Bus 2. San Sigismondo, on the Casalmaggiore road, is where Franceso Sforza married Bianca Visconti in 1441, a union that increased the prosperity of Cremona. The present, beautifully frescoed, church was built in 1463 to commemorate the marriage and replaced the original building.

TAKING A BREAK

Try **Pasticceria Duomo** at 6 Via Bocaccino, near the cathedral, for coffee and pastries. For a meal there are several excellent restaurants in Via Sicardo, close to the baptistery.

✚ 197 F1
Torrazzo
🕐 Jun–Sep Tue–Sun 10.30–1, 2.30–5.30; Oct–May 10–1 💶 Moderate

Palazzo del Comune
☎ 0372 22138 🕐 Mon–Sat 9–6, Sun 10–6 💶 Moderate. Entrance tickets for the Saletta dei Violini must be bought at the bookshop in the courtyard

Museo Civico
☎ 0372 407770 🕐 Tue–Sat 9–6, Sun 10–6 💶 Expensive

CREMONA: INSIDE INFO

Top tip A recording of the famous violins is played in the **Saletta dei Violini**, but you can arrange to attend when the violins are played to keep them tuned.

Mantova

South of Peschiera del Garda, Lake Garda's outflowing river, the Mincio, runs into low-lying, swampy ground. Here it languidly turns right, forming three lagoons. In the well-protected space between these sits Mantova (also known as Mantua), birthplace of Virgil in around 70 BC and seat of the art-loving Gonzaga family.

The Gonzagas ruled Mantova for 300 years from 1328, making it a centre for art and learning: Andrea Mantegna was court artist for 46 years until his death and Titian was a regular visitor. Gonzaga rule left much to admire, but after the Habsburgs deposed them the city became a military centre.

Palazzo Ducale

If you have driven south along the A22 from Verona and exited at Mantova Nord you will enter the city along Via Legnago, crossing a bridge between Lago di Mezzo (right) and Lago Inferiore (left) to reach the complex of buildings for which Mantova is famed. Here, on the eastern side of Piazza Sordello, is the Palazzo Ducale.

Begun before Gonzaga rule, but extended by them, the rather ordinary façade disguises a Renaissance masterwork. The Corte Vecchia dates from the 13th century, with Gonzaga additions by successive rulers. As well as palatial rooms, the Gonzagas added the Basilica di Santa Barbara and the Castello di San Giorgio, which houses the complex's most famous room. Sadly, the great art collection of the Gonzagas – most of it collected by Isabella d'Este, wife of Francesco II Gonzaga – was sold off in the 1620s to settle mounting debts. Most of

The medieval Piazza delle Erbe is lit up at nightfall

the finest works went to Charles I of England. The art that remains, though good, is hardly breathtaking. The same cannot be said of the palazzo's sumptuously decorated rooms. They are all magnificent, but the Camera degli Sposi, in the Castello, is the highlight for its frescoes by Mantegna. These includes life-like portraits of the Gonzaga, which give a real feeling for Renaissance courtly life.

Duomo and Piazza delle Erbe

Across from the Palazzo Ducale are Mantova's Duomo, an unattractive 18th-century building, and two even less attractive palazzos. To the southeast, look out for the niche statue of Virgil. To the left are the Renaissance Palazzo della Ragione and the 11th-century Rotonda di San Lorenzo. To the right is the **Basilica Sant'Andrea** (entrance in Piazza Mantegna, a continuation of Piazza delle Erbe), a superb 15th-century building by Leon Battista Alberti housing a Holy Relic and the tomb of Mantegna.

As with all things Italian, weddings in Mantova are very stylish

Continue along Via Roma, Via Amedeo and Via Acerbi to **Casa di Mantegna**, a brick house with a circular courtyard designed by the artist.

On again is **Palazzo Te**, the summer villa of the Gonzagas, built by Giúlio Romano in the early 16th century. The rooms here compare with anything in the Palazzo Ducale.

TAKING A BREAK

Mantova is famous for its local cuisine, including *stracotto di asino* (donkey stew) and a garlic salami that can make your eyes water. Try the former at **Due Cavallini**, at Via Salnitro 5. The latter is best purchased and eaten in private: try **Panificio Freddi** at Piazza Cavallotti 7.

✚ 198 C1
Palazzo Ducale
☎ 0376 352100 🕐 Tue–Sun 8.45–7.15 (last ticket 6.30). Most rooms open on guided tour only, reservation advised, tel 041 2411897 💷 Expensive

Basilica Sant' Andrea
🕐 Mon–Fri 10.30–12, 3–7, Sat 10.30–12, 3–6, Sun 11.45–12.15, 3–5
💷 Free 🚫 No photography

Casa di Mantegna
☎ 0376 360506/326685 🕐 Tue–Sat 10–1, 3–6, Sun 10–6 💷 Moderate

Palazzo Te
☎ 0376 323266 🕐 Mon 1–6, Tue–Sun 9–6 (last ticket 5.30) 💷 Expensive

Vicenza

Renowned as the city of Andrea Palladio, Vicenza is an open-air museum to one of the world's greatest architects, a man whose work has influenced successive generations.

Corso Palladio

To see some of Palladio's greatest and most influential works follow Corso Palladio from Porta Castello. To the right, across Piazza del Castello, is Palazzo Breganze, then to the left is Palazzo Bonin Thiene. Left again, in Corso Fogazzoro, is Palazzo Valmarana-Braga. The list seems almost endless, but to see the best keep walking, reaching, at the street's end, Piazza Matteotti and the Palazzo Chiericati to the right and the Teatro Olimpico to the left. The palazzo was built in the 1550s (though not completed for 100 years) and is considered by many to be Palladio's masterpiece. Today it houses the city's **Pinacoteca** (art gallery), with works by Tintoretto, Tiepolo and Veronese. The **Teatro Olimpico** was Palladio's last great work and is the oldest operating indoor theatre in the world. The first play here was Sophocles' *Oedipus Rex*, staged in 1585.

The Basilica Palladiana dominates the view of Vicenza

VICENZA: INSIDE INFO

Top tip A **combined entrance ticket, the Vicenza Card,** is available for all the city's main attractions.
• If the **Palladio villas** are your main interest, do not come in winter as most of them are shut from November to March.

Hidden gem Vicenza is a centre for Italian **gold-working,** with many craft studios.

Piazza dei Signori

About halfway along Corso Palladio, Corso Cavour heads off southeast, reaching Piazza dei Signori. Here the **Palazzo della Ragione** (often called the Basilica), with its double order of arcading with Tuscan, Doric and Ionic columns, is another of Palladio's greatest works. Here, too, are the **Loggia del Capitaniato,** Palladio's celebration of the victory at Lepanto, and a statue of the great man.

TAKING A BREAK

There are good cafés and pastry houses near Piazza dei Signori, and restaurants selling the Vicenza specialities – polenta (try it grilled) and salt cod – abound.

➕ 199 E3
Pinacoteca
✉ Palazzo Chiericati ☎ 0444 321348 🕐 Tue–Sun 9–5 (6 in Jul and Aug)
💷 Moderate

Teatro Olimpico
☎ 0444 222800 🕐 Tue–Sun 9–4.30 (6 in Jul and Aug) 💷 Expensive

Craft fair in the Piazza dei Signori, Vicenza

Walks & Tours

1 Monte Baldo
Walk

DISTANCE 8km (5 miles) **TIME** 2.5 hours
START/END POINT Lower cable-car station, Malcésine (tel: 045 592434) ✚ 202 D1

An exhilarating walk that combines rugged mountain scenery and a chance to glimpse alpine birds with panoramic views of the lake. Take a rain- and wind-proof jacket as the temperature on the ridge will be cooler than at the lakeside and thunderstorms can arise quickly on the ridge. The walk can be extended by continuing to the highest point on the Monte Baldo ridge, but this involves rugged terrain and should only be attempted by experienced hillwalkers.

1–2
Take the cable-car to the summit of Monte Baldo, ignoring the halfway station of San Michele. The cable-car has rotating cabins so everyone can enjoy the view of the mountain and Lake Garda.

2–3
Leave the cable-car and turn right, descending briefly (past a café) to reach an electricity sub-station and a path junction. Go straight ahead towards the ski-lift.

3–4
Keep to the right of the ski lift and follow the marked route 651 as it climbs over rough, then much gentler, terrain to a chair lift.

Cable-car
The *funivia* (cable-car) operates all year from 8am daily, the last descending car time varying with the month and weather – please check before ascending. The ascent takes about 10 minutes and cars run every 30 minutes. In the late autumn/early winter the system often shuts down for three or four weeks for maintenance, usually starting up again in time for Christmas. Winter (and summer, but to a lesser extent) running is weather dependent. A return ticket is €17.

4–5
The end point of the shorter walk is now in sight. Go through the fence into the nature

Walkers en route to the viewpoint on Monte Baldo

reserve and follow the clear path along the dwarf-pine-studded ridge. The grassy terrain gradually gives way to rougher ground, but the going is never very arduous and the path is always clear.

The objective of the short walk, Cima delle Pozzette, at 2,132m (6,972ft), is reached after about 1.5 hours' walking. On a clear day the view is breathtaking, extending west to Monte Rosa, and taking in the Adamello and the Alps north of it, and east as far as the Julian Alps. Inevitably, though, the eye is drawn to Lake Garda, laid out below the ridge.

The walk can be extended but – repeating the warning given in the introduction – this section is only for experienced hillwalkers. The extension adds 6.5km (4 miles) and a further two hours to the walk. The long walk is, therefore, 4.5 hours long, much of it above 2,000m (6,540ft) and half of it on a very rugged mountain with rescue for injured walkers several hours away. Please be very cautious.

5–6

Route 651 continues straight-forwardly from Cima delle Pozzette, dropping down almost 200m (654ft) then rising towards the summit of Cima del Longino (2,179m/7,096ft). From here the path becomes more rugged and spectacular, going over Cima Val Finestra (2,084m/6,815ft) then edging east around the cliffs of Cima Valdritta. It now becomes a true mountain path, experience and sure-footedness being required to follow the northern ridge to the summit of Cima Valdritta (2,218m/7,253ft), the highest point of Monte Baldo.

From Cima Valdritta, reverse the route, taking great care on descents, to Cima delle Pozzette and back to the cable-car top station.

2 Sirmione

Walk

The peninsula and old town of Sirmione form one of the highlights of Lake Garda. This short walk takes in the best the two have to offer, with fine views and historic places along the way.

DISTANCE 3km (2 miles) **TIME** 1 hour
START/END POINT Rocca Scaligera, Sirmione 🔲 200 C2

1–2

From the castle head into the old town, soon turning right into Via Dante, which is signed for the Passeggiata Panoramica. In Via Dante the lake moat surrounding the castle is to your right. Turn left, going slightly uphill – again following a Passeggiata Panoramica sign. Bear right (one more Passeggiata Panoramica sign) to reach a small garden, to your right. Go through the archway in the old town wall ahead. Beyond, to your left, is the Church of Santa Maria Maggiore (➤ 53–54).

2–3

Go down steps, turn right and down more steps to reach a gravelled area next to the

The fortified castle of Rocca Scaligera

lake. Follow the lakeside path ahead. There are usually black-headed gulls and mallards here as they have become used to being fed by visitors. On the lake you may also see great crested grebes. Stone seats are strategically placed to enjoy both the birds and the view across the lake to Monte Baldo. The path moves away from the lake, passing an area of rushes and tall grasses, with the occasional olive tree, to your right.

3–4

Go past the entrance to the jetty of the Palace Hotel Villa Cortine (strictly private – guests only). The gentle lapping of water on the shore is now the only sound to disrupt the peace. The yellow building to your left is the pumping station for Sirmione's spa water.

4–5

You will soon reach a wooden sign to the left pointing the way to the Grotte di

PUNTA
GROTTE

🔲 Grotte di Catullo

Catullo. The walk goes left here, but you can continue to the headland, passing the now dilapidated changing rooms of Lido delle Bionde (pizzeria and bar, pedalos for hire) to reach a rougher beach of flat rock slabs and pebbles, with unstable-looking cliffs to the left. It is possible to round the headland, but a fence stops further progress.

5–6

At the sign for the Grotte di Catullo, go up steps to reach a rugged path through an olive grove, bear right along a path and then take the steps on the left to reach a stepped path.

6–7

At the top of the stepped path turn right along Via Catullo, passing the Hotel Ideal on your left to reach the Piazzale Orti Manara. There are excellent lake views from here and the Grotte di Catullo (➤ 54–55) are to the right.

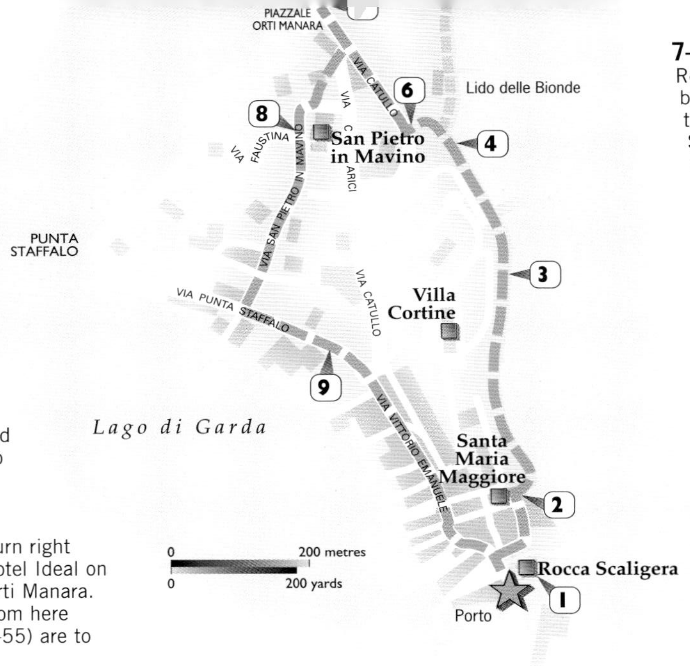

7–8

Retrace the walk along Via Catullo, but after passing the Hotel Ideal, turn right along a lane signed for San Pietro in Mavino. Follow this uphill through an olive grove, then turn right (still signed for San Pietro), bearing left to the church, where there is a cannon – it is now dedicated to the Italian military.

8–9

Ignore Via Faustina opposite the church and go straight ahead (or turn left from the church). The lane goes downhill, passing the Hotel Villa Maria to the left. At the crossroads turn left outside the Hotel Serenella.

9–10

You are now in Sirmione's main shopping area. Walk through an impressive archway, through another archway and bear left to follow the marble paving back to the castle.

Map labels: PIAZZALE ORTI MANARA · Lido delle Bionde · VIA CATULLO · VIA · San Pietro in Mavino · ARICI · VIA FAUSTINA · VIA SAN PIETRO IN MAVINO · PUNTA STAFFALO · Villa Cortine · VIA CATULLO · VIA PUNTA STAFFALO · VIA VITTORIO EMANUELE · Santa Maria Maggiore · Lago di Garda · Rocca Scaligera · Porto · 200 metres · 200 yards

3 Tremósine and Tignale

Drive

Above the northwestern shore of Lake Garda lie two high plateaux of alpine meadows. The road to them is twisty and occasionally tortuous but the views of the mountains to the north, mountain villages and Lake Garda are breathtaking.

DISTANCE 45km (28 miles) **TIME** 2 hours
START POINT Limone sul Garda ✚ 202 D2
END POINT Gargnano ✚ 201 D5

1–2

At the southern end of Limone sul Garda (➤ 56–57) is a large car park used by day visitors to the town. From this, take the route back on to the Gardesana Occidentale, the road that follows the western shore of the lake, and turn left towards the southern lake towns. Ignore the first turn on the right (signed for Tremósine) and go past a sign welcoming you to the district of Tremósine.

2–3

The Gardesana Occidentale now goes through a series of four tunnels. The first two are relatively short (about 100m/109 yards), the third is longer (about 500m/545 yards),

The village of Pieve, overlooking the western shore of Lago di Garda

the fourth about 2.5km (1.5 miles). About 100m (109 yards) after exiting from this fourth tunnel, take the road on the right signed for Tremósine and named as Via Benaco.

3–4

Go through a short tunnel, beyond which the road becomes very narrow, climbing steeply uphill with winding bends and hairpins to reach a *galleria* (an open-sided tunnel). Beyond this the road widens and offers the first view of the lake, to your right. Go through another tunnel, noting the arched roof: beware – if a lorry or bus is coming the other way it will be in the middle of the road. Beyond the tunnel the road becomes single track again with passing places.

A tunnel cut into the cliff face near the village of Pieve

4–5

This is a delightful section of road, with a stream in the wooded gorge to your right and a small bridge that diverts another stream over the road to fall as a waterfall beside it. However, the driving requires concentration and skill if you meet oncoming traffic. Patience and goodwill are required by both drivers.

Go over a tiny bridge to reach a section of road carved out of the mountain: the gorge here is very narrow. At a sign for the Hotel Paradiso (this really is beautiful country) a bridge appears ahead and above: you will actually cross this soon as the road doubles back on itself to gain height. Just beyond this the La Forra Ristorante is reached – a good place for an early coffee. The most tortuous section of the drive is now over.

5–6

The road now widens and soon you arrive in Pieve. The route bears right here (signed for Voltino), but it is worth stopping in the village to visit the Miralago restaurant, a good place for lunch. The restaurant is cantilevered over a stupendous drop above Lake Garda, so the views are amazing, as is the local cuisine. (To reach the Miralago, go into Piazza Fossato and, with the tourist office behind you, walk straight ahead.)

The tourist office has information on the Parco Alto Garda Bresciano, set up to protect the natural scenery of Tremósine and Tignale and the mountains to the north and west. The wildlife of the park includes roe deer, several varieties of frogs and toads, salamanders, the sulphur-yellow Cleopatra butterfly and, in the high hills, the European brown bear, which has recently returned to the area and is being monitored as part of the Life Ursus project, designed to increase its numbers.

6–7

Back on the drive, follow the road towards Voltino, with terrific views of the mountain villages of the Tremósine. Beyond Priezzo, where the church dates from the 7th century, the road is slightly wider and the countryside more open. Go through a short, single-track tunnel: the road now winds up to the village of Villa. Just outside the village there is a viewpoint from which to admire the terraced village and surrounding country.

7–8

Ignore a turning to the right (for Voltino and Limone), following the road around to the left and into Vesio. The road through the village is cobbled: a short stop is worthwhile as many of the village houses are very pretty and the Church of San Bartolomeo, built in 1760, is worth visiting. At the Y-junction beyond the village bear right towards Bréscia, Salò and Tignale, descending slightly through high alpine meadows with forested cliffs. At a crossroads – the first you have encountered – go straight ahead (again signed for Bréscia, Salò and Tignale).

Ahead now is a fine view of contorted rock strata. A 'Beware of the Deer' sign warns you that this is wild open country: please take care as the next section of road travels steeply downhill and has several hairpin bends.

8–9

Cross a river (the Torrente Campione) and start to ascend, again through a series of hairpins. The road then descends and climbs to reach a sign welcoming you to Tignale. Just beyond this you will have a glimpse of Lake Garda, and the road becomes a double-width carriageway for the first time. Ignore the road ahead signed for Tignale, staying with the 'main' road to reach a signed turn to the left for the Eremodi Monte Castello.

9–10

Turn left for the church. The road to it is single track and becomes steep. On the steep section the scored concrete surface suggests a difficult track in winter: it soon becomes apparent why, as a sharp hairpin is followed by a steeper section that leads to an archway barely wide enough for a car. Beyond, park in the steep, gravel area in front of the Church of Madonna di Monte Castello (▶ 57).

10–11

After admiring the church and the view from it, reverse the drive back to the main road,

look-
ing out
for the
roadside
shrines, with
frescoes of the
Stations of
the Cross, that may
have escaped your
attention on the drive
up, and turn left. Go
through Gárdola, bear-
ing left (signed for
Salò/Riva) and descend-
ing, with an expanding
view of the lake: there
are a couple of view-
points on the road
which can be used for a
fine view across the
lake to Malcésine, with
Monte Baldo rising
above it. Ignore the
turning for Plóvere, and
continue downhill to

regain the Gardesana Occidentale. Turn right and then left to reach Gargnano, parking in the centre for a coffee and snack at the Bar Azzurra in Piazza Zanardelli.

Plóvere is perched on the cliff edge near Tignale, on the west side of Lake Garda

4 North of Riva
Drive

North of Riva lie the huge spiky rock peaks of the Brenta Dolomite. An excursion there is a complete contrast to the waters of Lake Garda, and will usually require an overnight stay. On this drive you will be able to enjoy the rock scenery that has made the Brenta famous, but still be back in time for dinner.

DISTANCE 70km (43 miles) **TIME** 2.5 hours
START/END POINT Porta San Michele, Riva del Garda ‖ 202 D3

1–2
At Porta San Michele turn left on to Viale Dante, then right on to Viale Prati. At the stop sign turn right along Viale Giuseppe Canella. Now at the roundabout (Largo Marconi) take the second exit, signed for Varone/Tenno (Via dei Tigli). Bear right, then left, following signs for the Cascata del Varone and ignoring a left turn for Pranzo/Tenno.

2–3
Keep ahead along the road as it bears left, with a view ahead of

magnificent cliffs and mountains, and with a small vineyard on your left. You now start climbing uphill and will soon see the entrance to the

Cascata del Varone on your left (▶ 72). There is a picnic area and café here, but it is probably too early in the drive unless you are planning to view the falls.

3–4
Continue through Gavazzo, a picturesque village of old houses with shutters and colourful window boxes, going steeply uphill. There is now an expanding view towards Riva and the lake, with occasional parking places to take full advantage of it. The road ahead climbs through several hairpin bends, with olive trees and vines to your left and right, and the occasional orange tree as well.

4-5

Go through Cologna, with its beautiful church and campanile. Just beyond the village there is a viewpoint to your right: from here you can see Monte Baldo and the northern lake, and also enjoy more local views. The hillside is terraced for olive trees and vines, the terraces created by impressive walling. There is another picnic area on the right just before reaching Tenno.

At Tenno the old castle is now the Ristorante Castello, an amazing place to have lunch. Beyond, the hairpin bends continue, as do the marvellous views of the mountains either side and the occasional view of the lake.

appear to have been thrown into position. The church here has an excellent campanile.

Beyond, Lago di Tenno lies below to your right. Depending upon the weather the lake appears emerald green or turquoise blue – but at all times it is extremely picturesque. After a short descent through woodland you start to ascend again, the architecture now having a Tyrolean feel, though a frescoed church is a reminder that you are still in Italy. Another possible lunch spot – Pizzeria da Lalucio – is soon passed, and there is a picnic site just ahead on the alpine meadow.

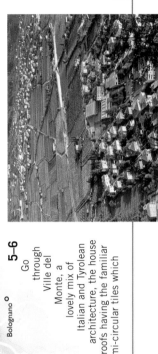

The view from Arco castle across the town

5-6

Go through Ville del Monte, a lovely mix of Italian and Tyrolean architecture, the house roofs having the familiar semi-circular tiles which

6–7

You now start to descend. Bear right towards Ponte Arco, ignoring the road to Faivè, and observe the impressive views of the jagged rock faces ahead. Go through Dasindo, a very pretty village, then notice, at Vigo Lomaso, that there are 'Beware of the Deer' signs. It would add another dimension to the drive to see one, but they are elusive creatures, and rarely seen.

Go past the beautiful Villa Lutti, with its curious round tower, and descend steeply through several hairpin bends to reach Ponte Arco. Turn right on to the road for Trento. To the left, the Al Pont is an excellent stop for a coffee or snack.

7–8

Drive through Terme di Comano – there is a spa to your left – and follow the narrow, winding road past overhanging cliffs to the right with the Sarca river to the left. On the next section of road you climb steeply with Dolomite-like cliffs and towers to your left.

Go through a very long tunnel, exiting to a view of mountains and huge rock faces before

Autumn colours are reflected in the waters of the lake

in summer and weekends only in winter.) Ahead you can now also see the castle at Arco, perched on a pyramid of rock. Bear right, crossing the Sarca again to reach Arco (▶ 82). If you are stopping in Arco, turn right after crossing the bridge to reach a handy car park.

9–10

At the traffic lights go left towards Riva. Soon you will pass a park with a fountain on your right. At the roundabout go straight ahead towards Riva, passing several garden centres. Go past a sign welcoming you to Riva. It is premature – there is still a little way to go to reach the town. Go straight ahead through two sets of traffic lights. If you are staying at the Astoria Park Hotel you will soon reach it, on your right. To the left, opposite the hotel, is the ultra-modern church of San Josep.

Continue in this direction to reach the roundabout where you turned off to Varone at the start of the drive. From here it is about 1km (0.6 mile) back into Riva.

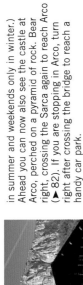

Alpine farmsteads are perched just below the tree line

plunging into another long tunnel, which ends with a galleria. There are further tunnels: after the fourth there is a picnic area on the left below impressive cliffs.

Now, as you start to descend into Sarche, there is a sign for the Zona del Vino Santo DOC with a list of *cantine* to visit should you wish to extend the drive. Sarche is famous among geologists because of the marocche, a remarkable area of huge boulders – glacial erratics deposited by a retreating glacier.

8–9

Cross the Sarca and turn right at the T-junction towards Riva del Garda. At the roundabout go straight on towards Arco/Riva, driving through a vast vineyard, left and right, which extends for about 2km (1 mile).

Recross the river and look out for the Castello di Drena perched on the hillside to your left. The castle was built by the lords of Arco in the late 12th century to defend the valley. The Arco valley is one of only a handful of readily passable routes through the mountains and the Arco lords had constantly to be prepared to meet invading armies. (The castle can be visited: it houses a museum of local history and is open every day except Monday

5 Local Vineyards

Drive

DISTANCE 80km (50 miles) **TIME** 3 hours, but longer if wine outlets are visited and lunch is taken
START POINT Tourist information office, Bardolino ✚ 201 D3
END POINT San Severo/A14 *autostrada*, Bardolino ✚ 201 D3

Close to Lake Garda's southeastern tip grow the grapes that create some of Italy's most famous wines, Bardolino and Valpolicella. There is a Strada del Vino through the Bardolino area, but the published map is not easy to follow, and the vineyards are in low-lying country. There is no 'official' route through the Valpolicella area. But the Valpolicella vineyards lie in much more spectacular country with mountains, woodland and expansive views. Here we take a route that links the two areas, making the most of each. The middle section of the route is passed in both directions, a necessary reversal to get between the two.

1–2
Start in Bardolino (▶ 79), at the tourist

Handpicking the grape harvest at Lazise

information office, which sits beside the Gardesana Orientale. From the office, head north (towards Garda), but almost immediately take the first right turn (Via Croce), which is signed for the Wine Museum (▶ 79). Ignore the sign for

the Strada del Vino on the right, continuing straight on and passing a sign for Affi with a fine row of trees to your right and a boatyard to your left: the first Bardolino vines are to your left after the boatyard. Continue through olive groves, soon passing Costodoro, a Bardolino vineyard, and then Frantoio, where local olive oil can be bought, with good views of the mountains ahead.

2–3

At the roundabout go straight across (on the road signed for Affi),

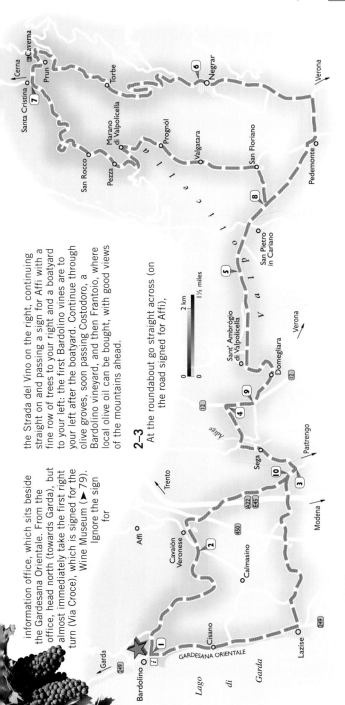

Huge wooden barrels are used in the production of wine

passing the Naiano vineyard: wine sales are available from the yellow building. At the next roundabout go right, passing, after 150m (164 yards), the La Canova wine sales to the right. Soon after, bear left along a road signed for Modena/Brennero A22 and Piovezzano, passing through olive groves to reach a little lake on the right. Cross over the A22 *autostrada* and pass the Effegi and Goretex factories to the left.

3–4

At the stop sign turn left towards Sant' Ambrógio di Valpolicella, looking out for some amazing stone boulders. Now, at the T-junction turn left, downhill, with good views of mountains ahead and Monte Baldo to the left. Go past the Stone Gallery, right, with its gigantic pieces of stone. The quarries of the Valpolicella produced the rossa di Verona marble from which many of the buildings in the city were constructed. Continue through the pretty village of Sega, then bear right towards the road (12) and go over the Adige River. Pine trees, cliffs and rock faces are now ahead of you, and the Lanza marble works are on your left.

4-5

At the T-junction turn right and drive through Domegliara. At the crossroads take the road left signed San Ambrógio and Negrar and after about 100m (109 yards) (go under a railway bridge and slightly uphill) turn right towards Negrar/San Pietro in Cariano.

Continue uphill, with lovely large houses to your left and good views. Go straight ahead at the traffic lights and under a bridge. Your first Valpolicella vineyard is to your right with terraced vineyards to your left. Go under another bridge. There are excellent views of Monte Baldo from this section of road.

5-6

Go straight ahead at the roundabout (signed San Pietro in Cariano/Pedemonte) and again at the traffic lights. Do not bear left with the road but keep going ahead (leaving the main road) past the Famila supermarket on your right, with more vineyards to both left and right. The road narrows just before a stop sign: turn right at the traffic lights following the sign for Negrar. After passing shops, turn left at the traffic lights. There are beautiful views here, with Monte Baldo on your left and forested hills to your right. The Cantina Sociale on your left is a Valpolicella organization and sells local wines. Go through Negrar – a pretty village with a picturesque 12th-century church and campanile – to your left and a river to your right.

6-7

Look out for a left turn signed for Prun/Torbe. The Osteria Nuova Pizzeria, immediately on your right as you turn, is excellent for a short break or for lunch. The road beyond rises steeply through a series of hairpins with excellent views all around. Go through the picturesque village of Torbe, and continue uphill. Bear left towards Cerna/Santa Cristina, soon passing incredible marble quarries to the right. The stone has been obtained by excavating into the mountain to form a series of caverns. Long abandoned and now unwholesome, the caverns are not pleasant to enter, but the view into them is extraordinary.

7-8

At the stop sign, turn left for Marano di Valpolicella. Soon you pass a picnic area to the left, with stone tables and seats. There are excellent views of woodland here and as the road is usually very quiet this could be an alternative lunch spot. Back on the road, as you descend there are spectacular views to forested mountainside. Continue downhill, passing a lake, through the village of San Rocco with balconied houses and a church with a fine campanile, then through Pezza, with views towards Verona on your left.

A series of downhill hairpin bends takes you to Marano di Valpolicella, with its vast domed church. Go through Prognól and Valgatara, passing the San Rustico and Michele Castellona wine outlets to reach traffic lights at San Floriano. A red light here allows time to admire the church and campanile ahead. Turn right, soon passing the Ceseri wine outlet and rejoining the outward route close to the Famila supermarket.

8-9

Go straight over at the roundabout to reverse the drive through San Ambrógio di Valpolicella. Go straight ahead at the traffic lights (signed Domegliara), with excellent mountain views ahead. At the stop sign turn left (straight ahead is a No Through Road) and at the traffic lights turn right towards Pastrengo.

Vineyards are a significant feature of the landscape

9–10

At the next traffic lights turn left towards Pastrengo, passing a huge marble works to your right and a sign which marks the end of the Valpolicella. Go over a river bridge, then bear left on a road signed for Pastrengo/Lazise. Go uphill, then bear right towards Lazise.

10–1

Bear left at the Y-junction, heading towards Lazise. Cross the A22 *autostrada*, with final views of Monte Baldo beyond the conifers on your right. Go past the Bardolino vineyards of Ca' Furia, Podere San Giorgio and Girasole (to your right), then turn left towards Lazise. The Azienda Agricola della Pieve – olive oil sales and an *agriturismo* site – is to your left. Go under a bridge with a little lake on your left, passing through Montiana. This section of the route passes through pleasant country and you soon have your first glimpse of Lake Garda. At the stop sign turn right to reach Lazise (➤ 79), following the lakeside road north from there to return to Bardolino.

Practicalities

GETTING ADVANCE INFORMATION

Websites
- Italian State Tourist Board: www.enit.it
- Italian Tourist Office for US: www.italiantourism.com
- Bergamo: www.provincia.bergamo.it
- Bréscia: www.bresciatourism.it
- Lake Como: www.lakecomo.com
- Lake Garda: www.gardalake.it
- Verona: www.tourism.verona.it

BEFORE YOU GO

WHAT YOU NEED

		UK	Germany	USA	Canada	Australia	Ireland	Netherlands	Spain
●	Required								
○	Suggested								
▲	Not required								
△	Not applicable								

Some countries require a passport to remain valid for a minimum period (usually at least six months) beyond the date of entry – contact their consulate or embassy or your travel agent for details.

	UK	Germany	USA	Canada	Australia	Ireland	Netherlands	Spain
Passport/National Identity Card	●	●	●	●	●	●	●	●
Visa (regulations can change – check before booking your trip)	▲	▲	▲	▲	▲	▲	▲	▲
Onward or Return Ticket	○	○	●	●	●	○	○	○
Health Inoculations (tetanus and polio)	▲	▲	▲	▲	▲	▲	▲	▲
Health Documentation	●	●	▲	▲	▲	●	●	▲
Travel Insurance	○	○	○	○	○	○	○	○
Driver's Licence (national)	●	●	●	●	●	●	●	●
Car Insurance Certificate	●	●	●	●	●	●	●	●
Car Registration Document	●	●	●	●	●	●	●	●

WHEN TO GO

Riva

High season   Low season

JAN	FEB	MAR	APR	MAY	JUN	JUL	AUG	SEP	OCT	NOV	DEC
4°C	7°C	11°C	14°C	18°C	22°C	25°C	24°C	19°C	15°C	10°C	6°C
39°F	45°F	52°F	57°F	64°F	72°F	77°F	75°F	66°F	59°F	50°F	43°F

Sun   Cloud   Sun/Showers

Italy's climate is **predominantly Mediterranean**, but in the north the proximity of the Alps tempers the heat of summer, while the lakes, acting like giant storage radiators, take the edge off the cold of winter. The result is one of the most invigorating climates in Europe, a fact not lost on 19th-century royalty, who headed this way to build villas.

Summer days can be hot, but are more usually comfortably warm. If the temperature does soar, the breezes generated by the lakes are always on hand to relieve the heat. In winter there can be rain and fog, and there can also be snow, but this is usually confined to the high ridges and adds skiing to the list of activities the area has to offer.

In the UK
ENIT
1 Princes Street
London W1R 8AY
☎ 020 7408 1254

In the US
ENIT
630 Fifth Avenue
Suite 1565
New York NY 10111
☎ 212/245-5618

In Australia
ENIT, Level 45
1 Macquarie Street
Sydney NSW 2000
☎ (02) 9392 7900

GETTING THERE

By Air Northern Italy has major airports at Turin, Milan and Venice, plus smaller connecting airports across the country. International flights from across Europe also land at smaller airports such as Verona, Bergamo and Bréscia.

From the UK, airports are served by Italy's international carrier, Alitalia (tel: 0871 424 1424; www.alitalia.co.uk), British Airways (tel: 0870 850 9850 in UK; 199 712266 in Italy; www.ba.com), bmi baby (tel: 0871 224 0224; www.bmibaby.com), easyJet (tel: 0871 750 0100; www.easyjet.com), and Ryanair (tel: 0871 246 0000; www.ryanair.com). Flying time varies from about 2 to 3.5 hours.

From the US, numerous carriers operate direct flights, including Alitalia (tel: 212 903 3575; www.alitliausa.com), American Airlines (tel: 800 433 7300; www.aa.com), Continental (tel: 800 231 0856; www.continental.com), Delta (tel: 800 241 4141; www.delta.com), Northwest Airlines (tel: 800 225 2525; www.nwa.com) and United (tel: 800 538 2929; www.ual.com). Flying time varies from around 11 hours (US west coast) to 8 hours (eastern US).

Ticket prices tend to be highest at Christmas, Easter and throughout the summer. Airport taxes are generally included in ticket prices.

By Rail Numerous fast and overnight services operate to Milan and Venice from most European capitals, with connections to Bergamo, Bréscia and Verona. Motorail services are also available from Berlin and Hamburg to Verona; from Berlin, Dusseldorf and Hamburg to Bolzano; from Calais to Nice for a relatively short drive east to the lakes; and from Denderleeuw (Belgium) to Milan and Venice. See www.trenitalia.it for details.

TIME

 Italy is one hour ahead of GMT in winter, one hour ahead of BST in summer, six hours ahead of New York and nine hours ahead of Los Angeles. Clocks are advanced one hour in March and turned back in October.

CURRENCY AND FOREIGN EXCHANGE

Currency The currency in Italy is the euro (€). Euro coins are issued in denominations of 1, 2, 5, 10, 20 and 50 cents and €1 and €2. Notes are issued in denominations of €5, €10, €20, €50, €100, €200 and €500.

Exchange Most major **travellers' cheques** – the best way to carry money – can be changed at exchange kiosks *(cambio)* at the airports, at main railway stations and in exchange offices near major tourist sights. Many banks also have exchange desks, but queues can be long.

Credit cards Most credit cards *(carta di credito)* are widely accepted in larger hotels, restaurants and shops, but cash is often preferred in smaller establishments. Credit cards can also be used to obtain cash from ATM cash dispensers. Contact your card issuer before you leave home to let them know that you will be using your card abroad.

TIME DIFFERENCES

GMT 12 noon	Rome 1 pm	USA New York 7 am	Germany 1 pm	Rest of Italy 1 pm	Australia Sydney 10 pm

WHEN YOU ARE THERE

CLOTHING SIZES

UK	Rest of Europe	USA	
36	46	36	
38	48	38	
40	50	40	Suits
42	52	42	
44	54	44	
46	56	46	
7	41	8	
7.5	42	8.5	
8.5	43	9.5	Shoes
9.5	44	10.5	
10.5	45	11.5	
11	46	12	
14.5	37	14.5	
15	38	15	
15.5	39/40	15.5	Shirts
16	41	16	
16.5	42	16.5	
17	43	17	
8	34	6	
10	36	8	
12	38	10	Dresses
14	40	12	
16	42	14	
18	44	16	
4.5	38	6	
5	38	6.5	
5.5	39	7	Shoes
6	39	7.5	
6.5	40	8	
7	41	8.5	

NATIONAL HOLIDAYS

1 Jan	New Year's Day
6 Jan	Epiphany
Mar/Apr	Easter Monday
25 Apr	Liberation Day
1 May	Labour Day
2 Jun	Republic Day
15 Aug	Assumption of the Virgin
1 Nov	All Saints' Day
8 Dec	Feast of the Immaculate Conception
25 Dec	Christmas Day
26 Dec	St Stephen's Day

OPENING HOURS

○ Shops   ● Post Offices
● Offices   ◐ Museums/Monuments
◐ Banks   ◐ Pharmacies

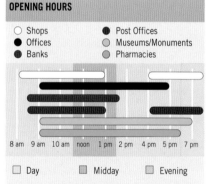

8 am 9 am 10 am noon 1 pm 2 pm 4 pm 5 pm 7 pm

□ Day   ▨ Midday   □ Evening

Shops Hours vary, but they are usually open Tue–Sat 8–1, 4–8; Mon 4–8pm. Shops in larger cities may open all day *(orario continuato)*.
Restaurants Usually 12.30–3, 7.30–10.30 pm; many close Sun evening and Mon lunchtime, with a statutory closing day *(riposo settimanale)*. Many restaurants close for the whole of August.
Museums Hours vary greatly, according to location. Most close one day a week – often Monday.
Banks Usually Mon–Fri 8.30–1.30. In larger cities branches may also open Sat morning and have longer weekday hours.
Post offices Usually Mon–Fri 8:15–2, Sat 8:15–noon or 2 (open all day in large towns/cities).

EMERGENCY 112

POLICE 113

FIRE 115

AMBULANCE 118

PERSONAL SAFETY

Petty crime, particularly theft of wallets and handbags, is fairly common in the major cities. Be aware of scruffy, innocent-looking children: they may be working in gangs, fleecing unwary tourists. If approached, hang on to your possessions, raise your voice and – if necessary – push them away. To be safe:

• Carry money in a belt or pouch.
• Wear your camera – never put it down.
• Leave valuables in the hotel safe.
• Stick to main, well-lit streets at night.

Police assistance:
 113 from any phone

TELEPHONES

from post offices, shops or bars. Tear the corner off the card before use.
When calling within Italy, simply dial the full number. Cheap rate is Mon–Sat 10–8. Hotels usually add a surcharge to calls from rooms. Dial 170 for the operator or 1240 for directory enquiries.

Telecom Italia (TI) payphones are on streets and in bars, tobacconists and restaurants. Most take coins or a phone card (carta telefonica), bought

International Dialling Codes
Dial 00 followed by

UK:	44
USA / Canada:	1
Irish Republic:	353
Australia:	61
Germany:	49

POST

Post boxes are red for normal post and blue for priority post (posta prioritaria). Most offices (posta) open Mon–Fri 8.15–2, Sat 8.15–noon/2. Stamps (francobolli) can be bought from post offices, tobacconists showing a 'T' sign and bars.

ELECTRICITY

Current is 220 volts AC, 50 cycles. Plugs are two-round-pin continental types; UK and North American visitors will require an adaptor. North American visitors should check whether 110/120-volt AC appliances require a voltage transformer.

TIPS/GRATUITIES

Tipping rates in Italy are low. Restaurant, café and hotel bills include a service charge so a tip is not expected, although many people leave a few coins in restaurants, and up to 10 per cent in smart ones.

Taxis	Round up to nearest €0.50
Tour guides	Discretion
Porters	€0.50–€1 per bag
Chambermaids	€0.50–€1 per day
Bar service	Up to €0.25
Lavatory attendants	Small change

CONSULATES and EMBASSIES

UK	**USA**	**Ireland**	**Australia**	**New Zealand**
☎ 06 4220 0001	☎ 06 46 741	☎ 06 697 9121	☎ 06 852 721	☎ 06 441 7171

HEALTH

Insurance Nationals of EU countries can get medical treatment at reduced cost in Italy with the relevant documentation (on presentation of an EHIC card for Britons; contact the post office for latest regulations), although medical insurance is still advised, and is essential for all other visitors. Ask at your hotel for details of English-speaking doctors.

Dental Services As for general medical treatment (► Insurance above), nationals of EU countries can obtain dental treatment at reduced cost, but private medical insurance is still advised for all.

Weather Minor health worries include too much sun, dehydration or mosquito bites, so drink plenty of fluids, and wear sunscreen and a hat in summer. Insect repellent may be useful if you sleep with the windows open in summer.

Drugs Prescription and other medicines are available from a pharmacy *(una farmacia)*, indicated by a green cross. Pharmacies usually open at the same times as shops (Tue–Sat 8–1, 4–8, Mon 4–8pm), and take it in turns to stay open through the afternoon, late evenings and on Sundays.

Safe Water Tap water is safe. So, too, is water from public drinking fountains unless marked *'Acqua Non Potabile'*.

CONCESSIONS

Young People/Senior Citizens Young visitors and children under 18 from EU countries are entitled to free entrance or reduced rates to most galleries. Similar concessions are available to senior citizens over 65. A passport is required as proof of age.

Combined Entry Tickets If you are planning a lot of sightseeing in one area, enquire at the tourist office or at participating sites about combined tickets, which can offer much better value than buying individual tickets. For example, in Vicenza, a combined entrance ticket is available for all the city's main attractions.

TRAVELLING WITH A DISABILITY

Wheelchair access is improving in larger cities, but is almost non-existent in the rest of the country. In old towns, you'll find few pavements or dropped kerbs; streets can be narrow, cobbled and congested with parked vehicles. **In the UK**, Holiday Care (tel: 0845 124 9971; www.holidaycare.org.uk) publishes information on accessibility. **In the US**, SATH (Society for Accessible Travel and Hospitality; www.sath.org) has lots of tips for travellers with visual impairment or reduced mobility.

CHILDREN

Most bars and restaurants welcome children, but few have baby-changing facilities.

TOILETS

There are public toilets at railway stations, in larger museums and in bars for customers to use. Ask for *il bagno* or *il gabinetto*.

CUSTOMS

The import of wildlife souvenirs from rare and endangered species may be illegal or require a special permit. Before buying, check your home country's customs regulations.

SURVIVAL PHRASES

Yes/no **Sì/non**
Please **Per favore**
Thank you **Grazie**
You're welcome **Di niente/prego**
I'm sorry **Mi dispiace**
Goodbye **Arrivederci**
Good morning **Buongiorno**
Goodnight **Buona sera**
How are you? **Come sta?**
How much? **Quanto costa?**
I would like... **Vorrei...**
Open **Aperto**
Closed **Chiuso**
Today **Oggi**
Tomorrow **Domani**
Monday **Lunedì**
Tuesday **Martedì**
Wednesday **Mercoledì**
Thursday **Giovedì**
Friday **Venerdì**
Saturday **Sabato**
Sunday **Domenica**

DIRECTIONS

I'm lost **Mi sono perso/a**
Where is...? **Dove si trova...?**
  the station **la stazione**
  the telephone **il telefono**
  the bank **la banca/**
  the toilet **il bagno**
Turn left **Volti a sinistra**
Turn right **Volti a destra**
Go straight on **Vada dritto**
At the corner **All'angolo**
The street **La strada**
The building **Il palazzo**
The traffic light **Il semaforo**
The crossroads **l'incrocio**
The signs for...
  le indicazione per...

IF YOU NEED HELP

Help! **Aiuto!**
Could you help me, please?
  Mi potrebbe aiutare?
Do you speak English? **Parla inglese?**
I don't understand **Non capisco**
Please could you call a doctor
  quickly? **Mi chiami presto un
  medico, per favore**

RESTAURANT

I'd like to book a table
  Vorrei prenotare un tavolo
A table for two please
  Un tavolo per due, per favore
Could we see the menu, please?
  Ci porta la lista, per favore?
What's this? **Cosa è questo?**
A bottle of/a glass of...
  Un bottiglia di/un bicchiere di...
Could I have the bill?
  Ci porta il conto

ACCOMMODATION

Do you have a single/double room?
  Ha una camera singola/doppia?
with/without bath/toilet/shower
  **con/senza vasca/gabinetto/
  doccia**
Does that include breakfast?
  E'inclusa la prima colazione?
Does that include dinner?
  E'inclusa la cena?
Do you have room service?
  C'è il servizio in camera?
Could I see the room?
  E' possibile vedere la camera?
I'll take this room **Prendo questa
  camera**
Thanks for your hospitality
  Grazie per l'ospitalità

NUMBERS

0	**zero**	12	**dodici**	30	**trenta**
1	**uno**	13	**tredici**	40	**quaranta**
2	**due**	14	**quattordici**	50	**cinquanta**
3	**tre**	15	**quindici**	60	**sessanta**
4	**quattro**	16	**sedici**	70	**settanta**
5	**cinque**	17	**diciassette**	80	**ottanta**
6	**sei**	18	**diciotto**	90	**novanta**
7	**sette**	19	**diciannove**	100	**cento**
8	**otto**	20	**venti**		
9	**nove**			101	**cento uno**
10	**dieci**	21	**ventuno**	110	**centodieci**
11	**undici**	22	**ventidue**	120	**centoventi**

200	**duecento**
300	**trecento**
400	**quattrocento**
500	**cinquecento**
600	**seicento**
700	**settecento**
800	**ottocento**
900	**novecento**
1000	**mille**
2000	**duemila**
10,000	**diecimila**

MENU READER

acciuga anchovy
acqua water
affettati sliced
cured meats
affumicato
smoked
aglio garlic
agnello lamb
anatra duck
antipasti
hors d'oeuvres
arista roast pork
arrosto roast
asparagi
asparagus
birra beer
bistecca steak
bollito
boiled meat
braciola
minute steak
brasato braised
brodo broth
bruschetta
toasted bread
with garlic or
tomato
topping
budino pudding
burro butter
cacciagione
game
cacciatore, alla
rich tomato
sauce with
mushrooms
**caffè corretto/
macchiato**
coffee with
liqueur/spirit,
or with a drop
of milk
caffè freddo
iced coffee
caffè latte
milky coffee
caffè lungo
weak coffee
caffè ristretto
strong coffee
calamaro squid
cappero caper
carciofo
artichoke
carota carrot
carne meat
carpa carp

casalingo
home-made
cassata
Sicilian fruit
ice-cream
cavolfiore
cauliflower
cavolo cabbage
ceci chickpeas
cervello brains
cervo venison
cetriolino
gherkin
cetriolo
cucumber
cicoria chicory
cinghiale boar
cioccolata
chocolate
cipolla onion
coda di bue
oxtail
coniglio rabbit
contorni
vegetables
coperto
cover charge
coscia
leg of meat
cotolette cutlets
cozze mussels
crema custard
crostini canapé
with savoury
toppings or
croutons
crudo raw
digestivo after-
dinner liqueur
dolci cakes/
desserts
erbe aromatiche
herbs
fagioli beans
fagiolini
green beans
fegato liver
faraona
guinea fowl
facito stuffed
fegato liver
finocchio fennel
formaggio
cheese
forno, al baked
frittata omelette
fritto fried
frizzante fizzy
frulatto whisked

frutti di mare
seafood
frutta fruit
funghi
mushrooms
gamberetto
shrimp
gelato ice-cream
ghiaccio ice
gnocchi potato
dumplings
granchio crab
gran(o)turco
corn
griglia, alla
grilled
imbottito
stuffed
insalata salad
IVA VAT
latte milk
lepre hare
lumache snails
manzo beef
merluzzo cod
miele honey
minestra soup
molluschi
shellfish
olio oil
oliva olive
ostrica oyster
pancetta bacon
pane bread
panna cream
parmigiano
Parmesan
passata sieved
or creamed
pastasciutta
dried pasta
with sauce
pasta sfoglia
puff pastry
patate fritte
chips
pecora mutton
pecorino
sheep's milk
cheese
peperoncino
chilli
peperone red/
green pepper
pesce fish
petto breast
piccione
pigeon
piselli peas

pollame fowl
pollo chicken
polpetta
meatball
porto port wine
prezzemolo
parsley
primo piatto
first course
prosciutto
cured ham
ragù meat sauce
ripieno stuffed
riso rice
salsa sauce
salsiccia
sausage
saltimbocca
veal with
prosciutto and
sage
secco dry
secondo piatto
main course
senape mustard
servizio compreso
service charge
included
sogliola sole
spuntini snacks
succa di frutta
fruit juice
sugo sauce
tonno tuna
uova strapazzate
scambled egg
**uovo affrogato/
in carnica**
poached egg
**uovo al tegamo/
fritto**
fried egg
uovo alla coque
soft boiled egg
uovo alla sodo
hard boiled egg
vino bianco
white wine
vino rosso
red wine
vino rosato
rosé wine
verdure
vegetables
vitello veal
zucchero sugar
zucchino
courgette
zuppa soup

Atlas

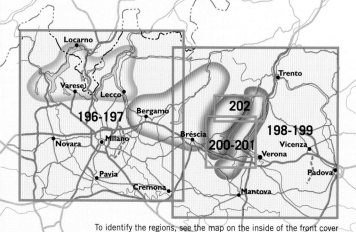

Locarno

Varese

Lecco

196-197

Bergamo

Novara

Milano

Pavia

Cremona

Trento

202

Bréscia

200-201

198-199

Vicenza

Verona

Padova

Mantova

To identify the regions, see the map on the inside of the front cover

Regional Maps

—·—·— International boundary	▣ Featured place of interest
—··—··— Regional boundary	▪ Place of interest
═══ Major route	✈ Airport
═══ Motorway	←——→ Cable car
━━━ Main road	▲ Mountain peak
── Other road	□ City
Built-up area	▫ Major town
National and regional park	o Large town
	∘ Town, village

196-199 0 — 10 km / 0 — 8 miles

200-202 0 — 4 km / 0 — 2 miles

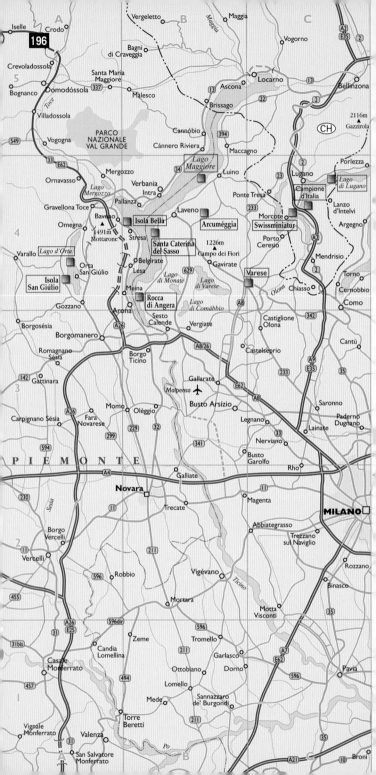

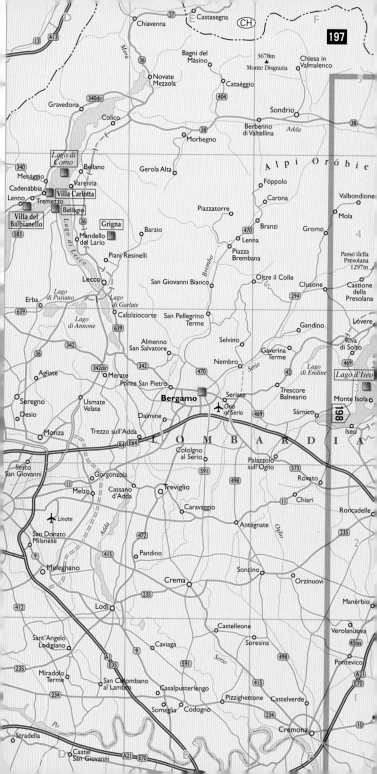

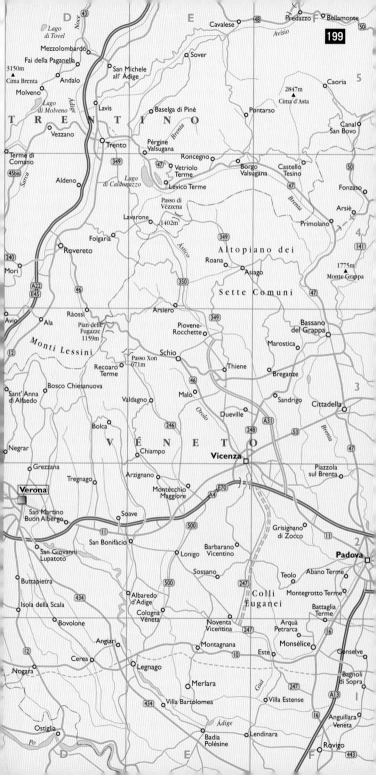

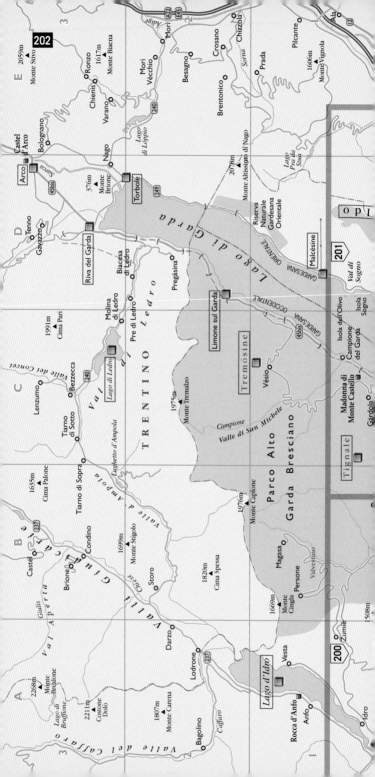

Picture credits

Abbreviations are as follows: (t) top; (b) bottom; (c) centre; (l) left; (r) right;
(bg) background.

The Automobile Association wishes to thank the following photographers, libraries and
associations for their assistance in the preparation of this book.

Front and Back Cover (t) AA/World Travel Library/A Mockford and N Bonetti; (ct) AA World
Travel Library/M Jourdan; (c) AA World Travel Library/A Mockford and N Bonetti; (cb) AA
World Travel Library/M Jourdan; Spine AA World Travel Library/A Mockford and N Bonetti.

Alamy 58t (Derek Payne); **Alinari/Roger-Viollet** (Racing driver Tazio Nuvolari) 2i, 5; **Archivo
GBB/Agenzia Grazia Neri** 26c; **Bridgeman Art Library** Min. Defense – Service Historique de
l'Armee de Terre, France, Archives Charmet 8, Vojenske Historicke Muzeum, Prague, Czech
Republic, Lauros, Giraudon 10; **EMPICS** Adam Davy 20b; **Gianfranco Fianello www.arena.it**
27tl; **Illustrated London News** 11cr, 23, 47; **Lebrecht Music and Arts** 21; **Marka** D. Donadoni
124; **Nature Picture Library** Phillip Clement 29b; **NPHA** Ingo Arndt 28b, Jordi Bas Casas 27b,
28b, Manfred Danegger 29b, Robert Thompson 27tr; **Provincia di Bréscia, Assessorato al
Turismo** 123; **Scala Archives** 9; **Science Photo Library** 24t; **Superstock** Wotek Buss/age
fotostock 119, 167.

The remaining photographs are held in the Association's own photo library (AA WORLD
TRAVEL LIBRARY) and were taken by **Anna Mockford and Nick Bonetti**, with the exception of
the following; **Pete Bennett** 22b, 57, 152t; **Steve Day** 137, 169; **Max Jourdan** 2iv, 2vi, 3b,
11bl, 17c, 20t, 43, 44, 45t, 49, 50, 54b, 55, 56, 58t, 60, 65, 69t, 70/71, 72, 74t, 80,
109, 112, 117, 118, 120, 121, 122, 132, 134/135bg, 134, 135c, 135b, 136, 141,
146, 149, 154, 172, 187; **Alex Kouprianoff** 190t, 190cl, 190cr; **Dario Miterdiri** 22t;
Clive Sawyer 2iii, 41, 150, 168; **Neil Setchfield** 14; **Tony Souter** 15.

Questionnaire

Dear Traveller
Your comments, opinions and recommendations
are very important to us. So please help us to improve
our travel guides by taking a few minutes to complete
this simple questionnaire.

You do not need a stamp (unless posted outside the UK). If you do not
want to remove this page from your guide, then photocopy it or write your
answers on a plain sheet of paper.

Send to: The Editor, Spiral Guides, AA World Travel Guides,
FREEPOST SCE 4598, Basingstoke RG21 4GY.

Your recommendations...
We always encourage readers' recommendations for restaurants, nightlife or shopping –
if your recommendation is used in the next edition of the guide, we will send you a FREE
AA Spiral Guide of your choice. Please state below the establishment name, location
and your reasons for recommending it.

_____

_____

_____

_____

_____

Please send me AA Spiral _____
(see list of titles inside the back cover)

About this guide...
Which title did you buy?

_____ AA Spiral

Where did you buy it? _____

When? m m / y y

Why did you choose an AA Spiral Guide? _____

_____

_____

_____

_____

Did this guide meet your expectations?

Exceeded ☐ Met all ☐ Met most ☐ Fell below ☐

Please give your reasons _____

_____

_____

_____

_____

continued on next page...

Were there any aspects of this guide that you particularly liked?

_____

_____

_____

_____

_____

Is there anything we could have done better?

_____

_____

_____

_____

About you...

Name (Mr/Mrs/Ms) _____

Address _____

_____

_____ **Postcode** _____

Daytime tel no _____ **email** _____

Please _only_ give us your email address and mobile phone number if you wish to hear from us about other products and services from the AA and partners by email or text or mms.

Which age group are you in?

Under 25 ☐   25–34 ☐   35–44 ☐   45–54 ☐   55–64 ☐   65+ ☐

How many trips do you make a year?

Less than one ☐   One ☐   Two ☐   Three or more ☐

Are you an AA member? Yes ☐   **No** ☐

About your trip...

When did you book? mm/ y y   **When did you travel?** mm/ y y

How long did you stay? _____

Was it for business or leisure? _____

Did you buy any other travel guides for your trip? ☐ **Yes**   ☐ **No**

If yes, which ones? _____

_____

Thank you for taking the time to complete this questionnaire. Please send it to us as soon as possible, and remember, you do not need a stamp (unless posted outside the UK).